Frank,

Good Luck
&
Good Selling

Lee Blackstone

MANAGE GLOBALLY, SELL LOCALLY

MANAGE GLOBALLY, SELL LOCALLY
The Art of Strategic Account Management

A. Lee Blackstone

IRWIN
Professional Publishing
Burr Ridge, Illinois
New York, New York

Senior sponsoring editor: Cynthia A. Zigmund
Project editor: Beth Yates

Designer: Mercedes Santos
Art coordinator: Mark Malloy
Compositor: TCSystems, Inc.
Typeface: 11/14 Palatino
Printer: Book Press

Library of Congress Cataloging-in-Publication Data

Blackstone, A. Lee.
    Manage globally, sell locally : the art of strategic account
management / A. Lee Blackstone.
        p.   cm.
    Includes index.
    ISBN 0-7863-0330-1
    1. Selling—Key accounts.   2. Marketing—Key accounts.   3. Sales
management.   I. Title.
    HF5438.8.K48B58   1995
    658.85—dc20   94–11218

Printed in the United States of America
1 2 3 4 5 6 7 8 9 0 BP 1 0 9 8 7 6 5 4

To my wife Linda; she is my sounding board and my conscience.

To my daughter Shannon, my sometimes editor, sometimes graphic artist, and all times critic.

To my daughter Ivy; she helps out at all the right times.

To my daughter Lindsay; she brightens my every day.

To my partner Frank Cullen, for the endless efforts he puts forth.

To you, and to your success.

Preface

This is not a book on basic sales. It is not about sales management. Its thesis is that the migration to account-focused selling is already moving at a pace few can keep up with. Many traditional territory selling approaches are still being used. Those ideas, however popular, will become ineffective, if not detrimental.

In recent decades we have witnessed a dramatic shift in the deployment of the sales force. The shift is from territory-based to account-focused salespeople, and they need to share information globally. Relationship management has become the mainstay of success. The gathering and translation of account strategy into operational plans lead to a sustained competitive advantage. It is no longer a battle with purchasing agents; it is an understanding of the customer's strategic business objectives and what you can do to help your customer attain them.

There is a great temptation, given the extensive materials available from diverse sources, to employ account-focused selling techniques based on the traditional territory-based approach. The day-to-day tactical activities of an account manager parallel those of a territory-based sales rep but also require a broader understanding of business strategies. The coupling of the strategic and tactical approaches to account management will clearly win in the long run.

This book is intended for the person who is managing a small number of accounts. We expand on the traditional how-to approach to address such issues as where to get accounts, key contacts, and competitive intelligence, why you need them, and how to develop and implement a successful operational plan.

Remember, I am more concerned about your being successful than you are.

This book is for those of you who want to contribute to your customer's success. By definition, if the customer is successful, then so are you. If you don't like selling goods at the lowest cost or making the weekly call on the purchasing department, you have two choices: change the way you are selling, or lose your account to someone who is truly concerned about helping the customer succeed.

If there is any question about account-focused sales and management, just remember: Territories and markets don't issue purchase orders; companies issue purchase orders. Those who do the best job of managing the relationships between the companies and between the people and who make sure that sales opportunities, projects, and commitments are all successfully delivered will ultimately win.

Here's to you—the winners!

A. Lee Blackstone

Introduction

This book discusses global account management and localized selling from a contemporary perspective.

The book begins with relationship management and the differences between the sales cycle and the one critical aspect of sales: the customer's buying cycle. As the account-development process evolves and the importance of managing personal relationships increases, a set of definitions are needed to effect concise communications. Chapter 4 discusses the transition to strategic account management, which is clearly laid out in a graphical format. You will have to continue to sell the relationship to the customer as well as internally. Chapters 5 and 6 discuss what is necessary to prepare for your briefing to your executive management.

As you begin to implement the strategic account plan, you will undoubtedly be dealing with a new group of customer executives. This book will show you which questions you are likely to be asked by a customer executive, which questions you can ask them to increase your credibility, and which questions your boss is likely to ask you when you return.

Chapter 8 shows you the right way to develop the appropriate relationships, and chapter 9 shows you what happens when you take your eye off the ball. Chapter 10 discusses how to eliminate prospecting and how to guarantee at least 70 percent of your quota before you go into the next sales year. Chapters 11 and 12 reveal how to eliminate account reviews and how to get your management involved in the success of the account. If you need to communicate with your customer executives, chapter 13 will help you do so.

If automating your sales organization is high on your list of priorities, chapters 15 and 16 identify the things that are essential. My consulting firm, Blackstone & Cullen, Inc., has provided software for the automation of sales forces since 1990, and here we reveal some of the secrets of how our customers have achieved a sustained competitive advantage.

Managing and selling to global accounts is tough. There is no easy way to do it, and it's hard work. This book is a tool kit of ideas. Use the ones you need to contribute to your customer's success.

If they are successful, you will also succeed.

Contents

Chapter One

The Strategic Account Manager

"The keys to successful strategic account selling are relationships, relationships, and relationships."

Gene Sherman, *Vice President, National Accounts,*
Pacific Telesis

Gene was absolutely right in saying that relationships are the cornerstone of long-term success in strategic account management. Gene's statement focuses on the relationship between people because, after all, people buy from people. Yet there are other relationships that must be in place. After several more hours of heated discussion, we finally boiled down strategic account management to its pure essence:

A *strategic account* is a client or customer that is pivotal to your company's success in a market. *Strategic account management* is managing the relationship between companies and between people and making sure that sales opportunities, projects, and commitments are all successfully delivered.

Account management is a process, not an event. It should be managed as a process and not as an isolated occurrence. The process applies to 1 global account with over 100 geographically dispersed reps or to 1 rep with

100 geographically dispersed accounts. The process is not derived from academic observation or consultative interviews but from repeated implementation yielding numerous successes.

THE SALES AND BUYING PROCESSES DEFINED

Most people think of the *sales process* in the following terms:

Understanding the need

Qualifying an opportunity

Proposing a solution

Answering objections

Negotiating price and contract

Closing the order

Making the delivery

Receiving the payment

More important than the definition of the sales process is the *buying process:*

Establishing need

Gathering information

Planning

Specifying

Purchasing

Implementing

These buying and selling processes go on every day. These are the processes vendors use to sell products and services and the ones buyers use to buy. They should not be confused with the process of strategic account management. Strategic account management is a much broader and more comprehensive process than just managing the individual sale.

Every large company operates with a business plan, a "map" of strategic and tactical direction. This global or companywide strategy sets the direction for the individual or strategic business unit. Each business unit must derive its own strategy from and support the grand strategy of the company. Once all individual strategic business units have a strategy in place, they begin to implement the functional and operational plans necessary to achieve these strategies' objectives. These plans may be classified as sales opportunities or projects. Once the plans are in place, resources must be assigned to them to ensure success. These resources are time, money, and people.

There are two sides to the equation: your company and your client company. Within your company, account executives are responsible for the relationship between the two companies. The role of the account executive is to uncover and communicate the client's strategies and sales opportunities and then to drive the process for ensuring a successful relationship at all levels. The account executive (AE) also has a coordination role. With a global account, the AE must be concerned with the overall account strategy and how to drive the development process worldwide. In the model shown in figure 1–1, roles are sorted out and responsibilities assigned. It is important to understand the roles of the various segments of the client organization and how to position yourself strategically for success.

There must be both strategic and tactical management of the account. Tactical account management has been go-

FIGURE 1–1
Managing Complex Accounts

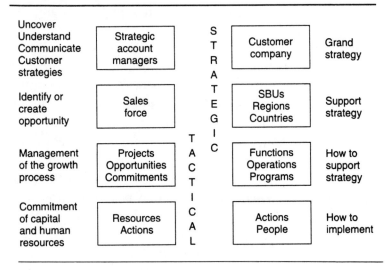

ing on for years. Simply stated, a sales rep's job is to carry a bag to a local facility and attempt to sell enough product or services to meet a monthly quota. But how does this activity tie in to the strategic management of the account? Many times the AE becomes a "scorekeeper" on what has happened and can't act as a process driver for future success.

The goal of strategic account management is to move the AE from the position of scorekeeper to that of the winning coach.

The American Heritage Dictionary defines the following words:

strategy   1. the overall planning and conduct of a large-scale military operation   2. the art or skill of using stratagems, as in politics or business   3. a plan of action

tactics   1. a device or expedient for achieving a goal   2. the technique or science of gaining objectives

To help make the transition from tactical thinking to strategic thinking, the AE must concentrate on doing a few things well. First, he must focus on managing the relationship between the two companies and the relationship among the people within the two organizations. In addition, he must manage how these people relate to projects, opportunities, and commitments. His job is to ensure that projects, opportunities, and commitments are successfully completed, that there are no surprises, and that everyone is happy with the relationships. At the same time, he should uncover enough new business opportunities to keep the funnel full.

The AE has the overall responsibility for managing the relationship between the two organizations. To do this effectively, the AE must understand the client's background, its overall strategy, its strategy by business unit, and how the AE plans to help the client. The AE must also understand her own organization and the specific opportunities, projects, or programs that will drive the account development. Once the opportunities or programs have been identified, a solid plan that requires both tactical and strategic attention must be put in place to ensure success.

Each step of the process will be developed in detail, and supporting strategic and tactical programs will be presented. It is also critical that the account development process drives the top line of the balance sheet and does not necessarily concentrate exclusively on cost reduction or productivity improvement.

FORCES DRIVING THE NEED
FOR CHANGE

The decade of the 90s and beyond will see global economics becoming more of a factor in business. Companies will have to meet increased expectations of their customers. The quality focus in the 80s has moved from being a point of differentiation to an imperative in the 90s.

Companies are reducing the number of their suppliers, intensifying their expectations of cooperation and partnerships in productivity. Companies also expect suppliers' decision makers to discuss key business issues with them.

The complexity of the business relationship continues to increase. Account executives need to be expert in more than just their product and company. They must understand global business issues and how these will impact their customer's business. This in itself is a tall order. There are very few salespeople with the background to be able to freely discuss these issues; there are even fewer that can take a global business issue and break it down into component problems that can then be dealt with easily.

Customers' buying power is being concentrated in a few locations to reduce overall expenses and personnel requirements. At the same time, traditional customers are feeling the impact of competing with global companies. A new set of rules is being drawn up on international competitiveness. The AE must be able to operate adequately in this new environment.

The companies that do the best job in global account development will reap significant rewards. Greater revenues, market share, economies of scale, and experience on the learning curve are several examples of these rewards.

These companies will also have the ability to "cherry pick" the best customers and deliberately give their competition the less-profitable and more time-consuming orders. This will lower the best companies' overall cost per order dollar and allow higher overall margins.

Chapter Two

The Four Phases of Account Development

The sales process involves a careful assessment of the customer's needs and then laying out specific projects and activities. In strategic account development, each customer may be viewed as a marketplace. Exxon, for example, is a market, not just an account, and as such should be segmented. Once it is segmented, specific projects or opportunities can be defined; the activities required to achieve them are then laid out, with responsibilities assigned. Key to the overall sales process is *the strategic account manager process*. The process is divided into four phases: Focus, Opportunity, Growth and Leverage, and Strategic Relationships. In figure 2–1 the objective is to establish a strategic relationship. But this is a step-by-step process, the first being the Focus phase.

FOCUS PHASE

The Focus phase is where the initial investment of time is made to assess the potential of a particular account and to decide whether it might be handled as a strategic account. Any subsequent investment of resources is a critical business decision. Therefore, the Focus phase should have a

FIGURE 2-1
The Strategic Account Manager Process

	Focus	Project/Opportunity	Growth & Leverage	Strategic Relationship
		Programs for opportunity Problem management	Top-to-top customer relations	Company is #1 in many SBUs/regions/countries
			Coordinate global functions Monitor geographic performance Review plans & strategies Review & set policy	Sustained strategic relationship Involved in customer planning process
				Dedicated account team
	Assign sales responsibility Monitor local performance Apply marketing expertise	Account management Commercial functions Focused sales responsibility Apply marketing expertise	Account management Commercial functions Focused sales responsibility Apply marketing expertise	Account management Commercial functions Focused sales responsibility Apply marketing expertise

$ Investment
$ Return

Phases

high priority, with significant executive involvement and support.

The goal of the Focus phase is to select the strategic accounts and determine their long- and short-term strategies by strategic business unit (SBU). The first step is to conduct a situation analysis. This may simply involve a one-day evaluation of the account or it may be a very detailed analysis. In assessing the sales or project opportunities, it is important to identify those that will provide the greatest return for the customer. These may not necessarily be the projects that bring you the greatest return. However, by addressing the customer's needs first, the AE will begin to establish the long-term relationship needed for success.

The second step is to use a revenue benchmark that will make the investment of resources worthwhile. This figure will vary by customer and by industry. For example, if you are selling welding supplies, the number may be $50,000, but if you are selling aircraft, the number may be $100 million.

OPPORTUNITY PHASE

In the Opportunity phase, the real test is whether an account can become a strategic account. At this time the foundation of the relationships between the two companies and between the people involved is being built. It is important to remember that this is an investment phase and that the cost of developing a long-term relationship around a sales opportunity will probably be more than a single order of equal value from a nonstrategic customer.

During this phase, the success of individual projects and the resources required to get and keep the business relationship will be assessed closely. If the cost of sales is lower than that of a normal account, then there are advantages to having this particular account as a strategic account; however, if the cost of sales is higher than for nonstrategic business, the investment should be questioned.

Another element of the Opportunity phase is the establishment of a project team. This is part of the investment and shows the customer that you are committed to the customer's long-term success. You must put your best people on the account during this phase because this is your customer's first impression of your implementation capabilities. If possible, the people who helped sell the project should be the ones who implement it. We highly discourage "bait and switch" tactics that are common but are becoming increasingly unacceptable.

GROWTH AND LEVERAGE PHASE

The Growth and Leverage phase is where your efforts begin to pay dividends. By this phase you have completed the first of many projects and are in a position to leverage your success. In leveraging your position, you must first protect the base of business you have in place by making certain that the customer remains satisfied. Next, you begin to search out growth opportunities within other segments of the customer company, and finally, you use your success to gain entry into new business units. There is one more critical element: When you landed your first sale, you displaced an incumbent vendor, whose AEs will be doing everything possible to recapture lost market share. Thus, you must have a competitive plan in place to counter any moves they may make.

During this phase you will begin to track individuals and create a detailed organization chart to assess the responsibilities and relationships of key customer personnel in various sales opportunities. There are two types of organization charts that you must use. One is the formal, hierarchical, standard organization chart that we have come to know and love over the years. The other and most important is the network diagram of the client, which shows political ties and mentor relationships. As you get closer to the client, you should begin to build your own Network diagram of the client's organization.

Here is an easy way to create your own network diagram. Use a spreadsheet such as Lotus 1-2-3 or Microsoft Excel and list in the first column and across the top row all of the key names in your client's organization. As you find out information about the relationship between any two people, enter it in the intersecting cell. You may use codes such as Mentor, Friend, Worked For, Dislikes, Worked With, Respects, and the like. In a short time you will have created an invaluable relationship/interaction matrix, or network diagram (see figure 2–2).

This type of information is built over time and becomes extremely valuable, just as background information on key individuals in the customer organization will be valuable. We will cover more on individuals and the type of information that can be collected on them in the Dossier section in chapter 3.

FIGURE 2–2
A Network Diagram

	G. Smith	F. Jones	L. Sampson	D. Green	F. White
G. Smith	x	Friends	Golf	?	Tennis
F. Jones	Friends	x	Same Club	Neighbors	Church
L. Sampson	Golf	Same Club	x	Worked For	Worked With
D. Green	?	Neighbors	Worked For	x	Mentor
F. White	Tennis	Church	Worked With	<Mentor	x

STRATEGIC RELATIONSHIP PHASE

The goal of strategic account management is to establish a long-term strategic relationship with your customer. When you reach the Strategic Relationship phase, you have the customer participating in your account planning process and you are participating in its planning process as well. You have earned the right to become part of your client's business success and are actively working with its executives to solve their business problems. By this time you are competing with a very small set of suppliers. A rule of thumb is that a client will only conduct joint planning sessions with one vendor per major business segment because they do not have the time to do more.

During this phase, increased top-level executive interaction occurs and may best be managed via a formal executive contact program or executive seminar program.

At this point in the relationship, dedicated resources are a requirement. Both sales and project-management resources must be part of the program. Some senior executives are reluctant to make the resource investment, but without it, you are doomed to failure. Some of your technical resources may even reside full-time on the customer's premises. These dedicated resources become the eyes and ears for your company; they are involved in the internal workings of your customer's organization. They should be protecting your base business while searching for new sales opportunities, leveraging successes, and maintaining the strategic relationship in those SBUs where you have developed one.

A great way to show your progress is to graphically describe how you are positioned within the client's organization. In figure 2–3 we have used Eastman Kodak as

FIGURE 2–3
Quantitative Benchmarks for Eastman Kodak's Divisions

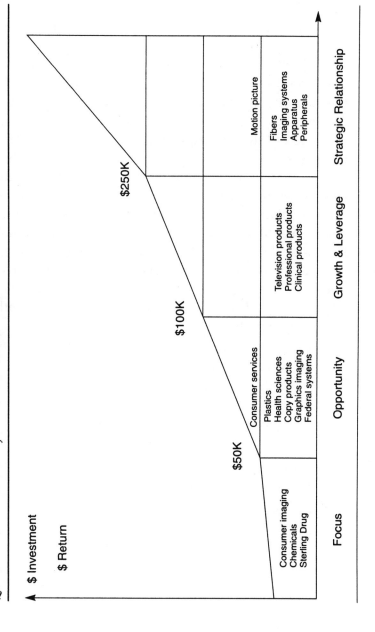

an example of how a company might be positioned both qualitatively (by phase) and quantitatively (by dollar sales). As with all examples, the quantitative milestones should be adapted to your specific industry and situation. When this type of chart is presented, your management team will readily understand your positioning within the account.

Figure 2–3 shows the quantitative benchmarks that have been set for various divisions of Kodak. The model shows that a strategic relationship exists in the Motion Picture, Fibers, Imaging Systems, Apparatus, and Peripherals divisions and that at least $250,000 in sales will result from sales efforts in each of these divisions. The Television Products, Professional Products, and Clinical Products divisions each show at least $100,000 in revenue generated, and so on. The model may be modified to fit your particular business, but it is a good indicator of position by division within each customer SBU.

Chapter Three

Understanding the Customer's Organization

One of the cornerstones of this book's methodology is the management of the relationships between people. Relationships take months and years to develop fully. You must win the trust and confidence of your customer over time; it is not an instantaneous event.

A look at any organization will uncover some type of hierarchical relationship between people. This relationship is commonly known as the chain of command and can normally be shown in an organization chart. Organization charts are very important to help you keep track of what is going on within the account. Another key piece of information you may want to ask for is a company telephone directory. Most customers are reluctant to give them out, but nothing is sacred in sales, so go ahead and ask. Just don't be offended if you get an occasional no!

There is also the informal "good ol' boy" network, where true influence lies. This is very difficult to chart. People in organizations have friends with "connections" who can make things happen for them. This informal network is the driving force behind many companies.

Management Level	Concerns
Senior executives	Can do
Middle management	How to
Technocrat	How to implement

The job of the strategic account team is to understand both the formal chain of command and the informal or internal political network within a client organization. Previously, information of this kind was undocumented and normally remained in the protected domain of the strategic account manager. For a strategic account team to function as a team, however, information must be shared across all levels within your organization. Certain restrictions, such as who can look at what information, will logically be in effect to protect the integrity of the information.

ORGANIZATIONAL CHARACTERISTICS

There are certain organizational characteristics that are common among all companies. The senior executives set the strategic direction of the company. This strategy is communicated to the middle managers, whose scope is partially strategic and partially tactical. The "technocrats" are the workers of the organization; it is their responsibility to implement the projects set forth by middle management.

When dealing with an outside vendor, senior executives are concerned about the "can dos" of the relationship. They will ask middle management such questions as, "Can this company meet our needs and expectations and do it in a cost-effective manner?" Once assured that this can be done, then the job of "how to" do a project is delegated to middle management. It is normally this middle-management group that makes the final decision on vendor selection, with the approval of senior management.

Middle management now redirects the concerns of "how to implement" a particular system or project to the technocrats, or workers. The technocrats can have a major influence during implementation, since it is their job to implement. If what you are selling is perceived as difficult to implement, the technocrats may exert a negative influence on your sales contact.

In planning the interaction with your client, it is imperative that you are prepared to address the needs of people at all levels in the organization. You must assure upper management that you "can do" the job. Middle management must be convinced that you know "how to" do the job, and the technocrats must be comfortable that you know "how to implement" the system and that you can help them do so successfully.

THE DOSSIER

Every person you deal with in your client organization wants to feel important, and in fact each of them is critical to the success of the account team. To make someone feel important is easy; just keep track of a few simple facts about them, such as which sports team they like or how their kids are doing in school. You can also build a dossier on key individuals. In addition to basic business information, family information, personal background, social information, employment history, and job responsibilities are key pieces of information that may prove invaluable over time. Gathering information on your key contacts takes time and is not something that you should plan to do over a week or even a month. Information gathering of this type is ongoing and never ending; it is a living, breathing thing that will serve you well over time.

Two other interesting uses of the dossier include using it to profile your competitors as well as your organization's people. In addition, if you are in a strategic account environment, chances are your competitors are also tracking your people, so why not keep tabs on their people and their actions as well? Just track your competitor as though it were a separate account and track its strategies, wins, losses, and people. Over time, insights on the behavior of your competitors can be mapped out.

Basic Information

The basic information on the individual customer includes name, address, secretary's name, department, title, and several phone numbers as well as E-mail address. Additional comments and notes areas should be set up as well. We suggest that you keep a copy of the biographical sketch provided by your client organization for this particular individual. It is also important to date all entries.

Additional primary information categories are also important and will be discussed individually. The first is family information, which covers detailed information on the contact's spouse and children. This may not seem necessary at first, but you will not find it uncommon for your top competitor to hire your best customer's daughter or son just to win the account away from you. If this happens and you do not actively track it, you may spend millions of dollars on marketing only to finish a close second and never know why.

Family Information

Keeping track of information on your contact's spouse may seem like a waste of time, but rest assured that this type of information can make or break your success in a social setting. You may want to send your contact a special note for her anniversary or, conversely, you purposely avoid involving your contact in a business meeting on her anniversary.

Information on the children is also important. Many times people talk about what their children are doing; this is a good way to establish a common linkage, especially if your son or daughter happens to be the same age, be in the same school, or play the same sports. If your customer is single or a divorced parent, it is important to know what child care arrangements are in place. This type of information helps you avoid awkward situations such as inviting the customer for an extended reference visit, only to discover that he has custody of young children and no one to keep them overnight. It allows you that additional touch of sensitivity.

Personal Background

Once information is obtained on your customer's family, the next step is the background of the individual. This begins with the high school and college your contacts attended and what they did while they were there. In addition to high-school activities and university details, other pertinent categories to track are advanced education, military, publications, organizations, countries lived in, and languages spoken.

Social and Civic Information

During your tenure in sales and marketing, you have probably attended a class that helped you identify the customer's style or personality and the things that are personally important to him.

More sales have been lost from poor social etiquette than from poor product performance. Being aware of information such as dining, drinking, and smoking habits will keep you out of trouble. If the customer is of a different political party than yours, then politics may not be a good topic for dinner conversation. If his personality is that of a "driver," then you can inform your management about what to expect. Should your company sponsor a golf or tennis outing, keeping track of the customer's level of play will ensure that he is paired with other players at the same level. Depending on the customer's religion, the choice of restaurant or the timing of business meetings during religious holidays can become a very sensitive subject. It's the small details that will carry you or kill you. Gathering social and civic information at least gives you a way to keep track of things you might otherwise overlook.

Employment History

A person's employment history gives you an idea of how she has progressed in the organization and how often she is promoted. Employment history can also span multiple companies. Someone who has not been promoted in the last five years may not be the decision maker you are looking for if your proposal would change the way the company does business; this person is probably not a successful risk taker. But if you are selling large volumes of commodities at a relatively stable price, someone who has been in a job for five years is probably the right person for you. Each situation is different and must be assessed on its own merits.

Individual Responsibilities

In addition to employment history, you should be aware of what the individual has accomplished and has been responsible for. If you are to be successful in working with various individuals, you should know their long- and short-term business objectives. If they plan to retire in six months, for instance, you may find you are dealing with a lame duck. Every company has a different set of performance evaluation criteria. By knowing how your customers are evaluated and compensated, you are in a position to help them be successful.

Additional responsibility details may also be important to your success. A customer's additional responsibilities give you an idea of what this individual has previously bought from your company, how the customer makes critical decisions, what issues were involved, where there are any known conflicts with management or any management priorities, and what the individual views as critical success factors.

Don't Be Overwhelmed

Remember, you are not expected to gather all of this information at once. It may take years to develop a complete background on a particular individual. Focus on the people you or your senior executives are likely to come into contact with first. These are the ones you should spend your time on. Other than that, go ahead and begin tracking all individuals you may be dealing with, and use the dossier as a phone directory and basic information log.

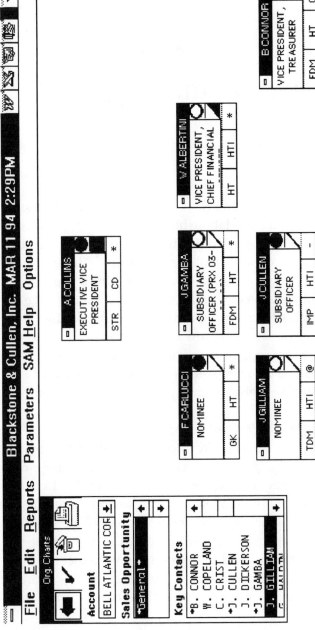

Blackstone & Cullen, Inc. MAR 11 94 2:29PM

File Edit Reports Parameters SAM Help Options

Org.Charts

Account
BELL ATLANTIC COF ▼

Sales Opportunity
General

Key Contacts
*B. CONNOR
W. COPELAND
C. CRIST
+J. CULLEN
J. DICKERSON
+J. GAMBA
J. GILLIAM

A.COLLINS
EXECUTIVE VICE
PRESIDENT

| STR | CD | * |

F CARLUCCI
NOMINEE

| GK | HT | * |

J GILLIAM
NOMINEE

| TDM | HTI | @ |

J GAMBA
SUBSIDIARY
OFFICER (PRX 03—

| FDM | HT | * |

J CULLEN
SUBSIDIARY
OFFICER

| IMP | HTI | — |

W ALBERTINI
VICE PRESIDENT,
CHIEF FINANCIAL

| HT | HTI | * |

B CONNOR
VICE PRESIDENT,
TREASURER

| FDM | HT | CC |

Chapter Four

Strategic Account Management

Are you acknowledging the fact that long-term success in selling is based on relationships, relationships, and relationships? More specifically, it is based on the effective management of two simple relationships. Those are between people and between companies. This is the essence of account-based selling. Historically, companies have organized sales forces by territory, industry, product line, account, key contacts, or any combination of these. In the future, the same approaches will continue, with some shift in focus based on what is in vogue, what the current economic conditions are, or simply who is setting the current strategy.

The shift in the 90s will be to account-based selling. This approach may be called key accounts, national accounts, global accounts, principal accounts, major accounts, corporate accounts, multinational accounts, and the like. Regardless of what it is called, its foundation is based on relationships. Figure 4–1 diagrams a process for building these relationships. The Executive box at the top of the model reflects the need for executive involvement in both companies. It also reinforces the need for the account team to discuss all aspects of the account with their executives.

FIGURE 4–1
The Account Management Process

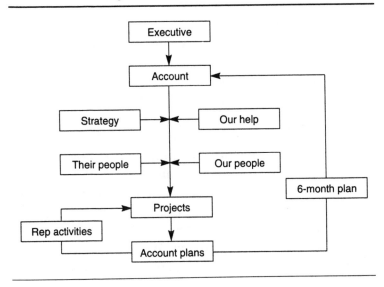

BUILDING THE RELATIONSHIP BETWEEN TWO COMPANIES

To build an effective relationship between two companies, each must believe that its future is based in part on the other's and that theirs is a partnership in success. Like all relationships, this requires that each has an understanding and appreciation of the capabilities of the other. To understand another company, the first must research a number of elements: global business issues, the other's mission and strategic direction, the impact of technology, growth areas, market conditions, and the like. Once you understand these elements, your company is in a position to help your customer achieve its business goals.

DEVELOPING THE PEOPLE

During my tenure as national sales manager for a software services and systems integration company, one of our key programs was account-based selling. We selected a number of accounts and began the process of growing the business. In one such case, I inherited a longtime employee (I'll call him Jim) who had a good understanding of the business and was eager to be part of the new program. Jim and I sat down and decided which account we should go after and began the process of segmenting the organization. We determined which divisions would most likely place the largest orders and which departments would allow us to make the highest profits. In addition, we mapped the competitive activity for all divisions and made a list of the people we needed to know. We determined that the overall market potential was about $200 million within this one account, so if we got it right, the rewards would be there. Our current level of business was under $1 million.

We prioritized the opportunities by the ones that provided us the greatest strategic positioning within the company and then began the implementation process. The plan included meeting one new department head in the client organization each week and having at least one strategic visit to our corporate headquarters each month by one of its vice-presidents. The business began to grow at a double-digit rate, but it had not exploded. Jim was doing an excellent job but was overwhelmed. As Jim was about to throw in the towel, the customer began putting an early retirement program into effect. Jim approached one of the senior vice-presidents and asked who, among those looking for an early retirement, would do us both the most good if they moved to our organization. Within a month, Jim had two new people on his team, both former department heads of our client company. They understood the client organization and who the key people were, and they had credible access to them. This set off the explosion we were looking for. Our business grew by 600 percent the first year and doubled again in the second year. Jim is now the vice-president of a very large part of the company, which is still experiencing double-digit growth through creative strategic account management.

BUILDING PERSONAL RELATIONSHIPS

Most successes are based on the relationship between two people. This is quite evident when salespeople are hired because of the business they can bring with them. But if you hire a sales rep solely for that reason, you are being somewhat shortsighted. If the rep came to you because you "bought" him, he will certainly go somewhere else for a few dollars more. A number of sales forces have been built on this mercenary approach and many have been quite successful—at least in the short term. Prime users of this method are construction and engineering firms and manufacturer rep firms.

Expanding personal relationships between companies requires leveraging one's presence. Relying on your key contact to introduce you to contacts in new areas is an ongoing process. Set a goal to meet one new department head every week and one new vice-president each month. It is amazing how fast the business relationship and the order rate will grow.

Once these personal relationships are in place, validation comes when the customer directs you to the projects without you having to prospect for opportunities.

MANAGING SALES OPPORTUNITIES

The effective management of sales opportunities is what allows you to remain the client's principal solution provider. It is tempting to go after the sales that provide you with the greatest short-term gains, and it is natural in a quota-based sales system. But there are other factors that must be taken into account, such as the following:

- Does this project provide the greatest return on investment to the customer?
- Will this project help them achieve their corporate strategy?
- Does the customer have the resources available to implement this project?
- Do we have the necessary resources to implement this project?
- Can we leverage this project across multiple divisions?
- Can we properly manage the customer's expectations?

Working in a complex sales process across a global account multiplies the effort required. You must now provide global account coverage and your people must communicate about the resources, issues, and results of each required action. To accomplish this, a process must be put into place to manage the account. Formally planning activities jointly with your customer at least every 90 days is mandatory. Lay out a plan covering the next six months on all account activity, with the understanding that you will update it every 90 days. This takes us to the Account plans box in the model shown in Figure 4–1.

ACCOUNT PLANS THAT EVERYONE UNDERSTANDS

Account plans can be as simple or as complex as the team desires, but there is one simple approach that everyone understands: the modified "to-do" list. Add two additional columns, issues and results, to the normal to-do list. Lay out a simple planning form, as follows:

Activity | *Who* | *When* | *Resources Required* | *Issues* | *Results* |

During the quarterly planning sessions, minimal time is spent on review by looking at the activity and at the results achieved. If you did what you planned to do, there is no need for elaborate review; if you did not, there is a need to focus on why that activity was not accomplished. This is a very simple but effective process to ensure that you are in sync with your customer and with your internal people. Experience has shown that a typical account planning session can be done in a half-day session, including interaction with the customer and five or six account reps. It is a proven process.

AVOID THE ACTIVITY TRAP

Traditional sales efforts take place in the Projects–Account plans–Rep activities loop shown in figure 4–1. Rep activities include contact management, quotations, proposals, expense reporting, forecasting, and so on. I love to compete with traditional sales organizations because, in every case, they are viewed as vendors and not consultative salespeople; they are competing on price and not value; and they are not concerned with long-term relationships but are probably relying on short-term relationships between the current salesperson and someone in the client's purchasing department. If this sounds familiar, you are in trouble. If your number one competitor has taken the time to understand the customer's business strategy and is working with key customer executives to help them achieve their goals, while you are focused on "selling stuff," it does not take a crystal ball to see that you are doomed in the long run.

PUTTING IT ALL TOGETHER

The following question summarizes the standards by which most sales managers are judged: "What did you do for me today?" Upper management demands performance and it can be difficult to justify the expense of developing long-term relationships when the return is not immediately visible. But when an order is needed to meet an end-of-month quota, the sales manager always goes to the best customers for help.

The transition to an account-based sales process will take two to three years; short-term sales might suffer, but in the end you will develop a permanent people-, company-, and opportunity-based strategic account management process. There is no magic—it takes hard work and focus. What follows is a "road map" or process listing points to get you there from here:

- Decide to focus on a specific customer.
- Determine that customer's strategic direction by strategic business unit.
- Determine what you are going to do to help the client executives become successful, point by point.
- Get strategic endorsement from the customer's senior management.
- Jointly plan the projects that give the customer the greatest return on investments.
- Plan appropriate activities to implement the project with the customer's involvement.
- Execute the plan, measure the results, and continue a rolling six-month plan, updated quarterly.
- Continually build personal and business relationships with your customers at all levels.
- Communicate openly within your organization worldwide.
- Allow input from everyone on the account team worldwide.

Follow these simple directions and you will find yourself with a solid foundation for account-based selling. Each leg of the relationship relies on the other for support. Step back and analyze your position. Have you put it all together?

Chapter Five

The Situation Analysis for Focused Accounts

In this chapter we will continue to build on the four-phase approach to the strategic account manager process. Each phase will be broken down and you will begin to see the how-tos and whys of the process. You will also be guided on preparing for discussions with upper management both in your organization and in your customer's organization.

The first step is to analyze a particular account. This means gathering as much of the right information as possible so an informed decision can be made on the amount of resources to commit to a particular account. There are six key areas for analysis:

- The customer and its financial strength
- The people and the organization
- Its market dynamics and business constraints
- Opportunities for short- and long-term business
- Competitive activity
- What we can do to make the client successful

To examine a customer in detail, there are several logical places to begin. First, if it is a public company, call its investor relations department and ask for a copy of the annual report and any other information that might provide insight into the strategic direction of the company.

Explain that you are the account executive for your company and that you need background information so you can brief your senior executives on the future opportunities for business between the two companies. You might also ask to be put on the customer's mailing list. Another reasonable request is for articles that have been written or speeches that have been made about the company or by its executives that might provide some accurate insight.

There is a wealth of information from on-line data services. Several good ones are CompuServe, Lexis/Nexis from Mead Data Services, Media General, and numerous industry-specific databases. A quick snapshot is Disclosure, which is available through several services and provides quick financial information. One Source provides a CD-ROM–based product that is updated monthly and contains much of the same information contained in on-line services; the trade-off is timeliness of data vs unlimited use for a fixed price.

Other sources of basic account information are:

- Stock analyst reports available from your broker
- Industry reports
- Business and trade magazines (several are available on-line)
- The *Wall Street Journal* (available on-line)
- Previous account sales reps and executives
- Information from old marketing plans
- Account plans and books
- Current contracts
- *Who's Who in Industry*
- *Scott's Industrial Directory*
- Dun & Bradstreet's *Directory of Corporate Affiliates*

- Press releases (often available on-line)
- Key contacts in the client organization

THE ACCOUNT PROFILE

Now there is a mass of paper on your desk, and you have to figure out what is important and what is not. After years of working with strategic account teams and programs, we have refined the information that is important to you, your executives, and your customer:

- Account name
- Address
- Phone number
- Number of employees
- Revenue
- Fortune 500 rank
- Industry rank
- Fiscal year ending date
- Number of locations
- Dun's number
- Standard Industrial Classification (SIC) code
- Main business
- Type of industry
- Major products
- Major markets
- Buying patterns
- Account manager's name, title, and phone
- Account mission statement

Everything is very logical and straightforward. The account

mission statement specifies the overall mission of the client. If your territory has a large number of accounts, this may be as much basic information as you want on a particular account. Additional information on financial condition would still be required, however.

THE STRATEGIC ACCOUNT MANAGER PLANNING PROCESS

Sales reps and managers are tactical by nature. They are driven by the constant pressure of meeting a monthly quota. All too often they view a sale as an event and meeting an annual quota as a series of events.

Salespeople with this mentality are likely to be hesitant when exposed to a process approach to selling. Using a process approach means viewing sales as a series of interrelated events. The *strategic account manager planning process* presents a logical way to view an account and to strike a balance between building the strategic relationship and meeting sales quotas. Most sales processes are viewed on a deal-by-deal basis; the strategic account manager is focused on the development of the overall account, including mission, strategy, tactics, positioning, and deals.

FINANCIAL INFORMATION

Financial information is important, regardless of whether it is for a small or large account. Your credit department will insist on it. A creative account executive will even ask the credit department to get a Dun & Bradstreet (D&B) report on an account and to become part of the account development process. A subset of the credit information will be used for executive presentations. The categories of financial information are:

- Gross sales
- Gross profits
- Net profits
- Assets
- Stockholders equity
- Market value
- Stock price as of (date)
- Price-to-earnings (P/E) ratio
- Earnings per share
- Long-term debt
- Research and development (R&D) expense
- Property, plant, and equipment
- D&B rating
- Percentage of sales spent on your products or services
- Availability of funding
- Buying cycle
- Lease vs buy
- Ancillary comments
- Last five years' sales history

Most of this information is directly available from a D&B report. Information on a lease may be obtained from 10K (Security and Exchange Commission Report) filings because most leasing companies require a UCC (Uniform Commercial Code) form to be signed by the lessee, which givesthe lessor preferential treatment in case of bankruptcy. This may be considered a liability and must be reported to the Securities and Exchange Commission

(SEC). It is therefore reported in the company's standard financial disclosure. The 10K also states what the lease was for and with whom it is filed.

GRAPHICAL INFORMATION

The next step in the process is to decide what graphical information you want to include in your account profile. Typical examples include earnings per share for the last five years, sales by business sector, maps, network diagrams, sales territory maps, Gantt charts, and organization charts.

As the account profile is prepared for the executives in your company, prepare as much graphical information as possible. Normally, an annual report contains several graphics that are appropriate and readily reproduced in various graphics packages and then used in your profile.

If you are dealing with several accounts located in one geographic territory, you may choose to depict the information by territory, perhaps aggregated by SIC code, industry type, or geographic subsegment.

YOUR CUSTOMER'S
MARKET DYNAMICS

To have the most impact on your customer's success, you should understand your contact's business as well as she does. This requires a lot of homework on your part or, better yet, asking your contact many questions about her business. As a first step for any business relationship, take a tour of your customer's facility. It makes no difference whether it is a bank, insurance company, brokerage house, manufacturing facility, or warehouse. You need to walk around and understand how the customer's business works physically. Bring a tape recorder with you (assuming your customer approves), and take notes verbally as you go. If you ask questions about the operation, many times additional sales opportunities will surface. Ask specifically about any bottlenecks in the operation or critical areas in the process. Deriving solutions to bottlenecks or smoothing out critical areas in the process will almost always result in a sale.

As the evaluation of your customer's business progresses, there are a number of business areas that you should understand. The following list gives you an idea of the areas to focus on. This list is not exhaustive and should be expanded or customized to accommodate your particular customer.

- Market conditions
- Market tactics
- Market trends
- Key customers
- Distribution channels
- Critical success factors
- Competitors
- Competitive tactics
- Competitive trends

DETERMINING YOUR CUSTOMER'S BUSINESS CONSTRAINTS

There are a number of factors outside your control that could have a dramatic effect on your business. These factors typically impact your customer as well. They include legal, community, social, environment, regulatory, and government factors.

These are strategic issues and will give your senior executives several topics for discussion during executive visits. As you become more involved with your own senior executives and those of your client organization, you will have to prepare a vast amount of background information on your account prior to an executive visit. This task will be very straightforward if you use the strategic account manager process described in Chapter 2. You must understand your customer's strategy and your own company's strategy, and you should be able to articulate both. In addition, an understanding of the difficult issues facing each company will allow you to brief your executives on the likely topics for discussion.

STRATEGIC BUSINESS UNITS

If the account you are working with has multiple strategic business units (SBUs), then you need to get information on each of them. A good place to begin is the D&B *Handbook of Corporate Affiliates*, which is often referred to as the Red Book. It contains location information for the subsidiaries of most companies; however, it does not list every subsidiary location. These must be obtained from your customer, and in many cases its purchasing department has compiled a list of every location of every division.

As you might imagine, if you are dealing with a highly diversified company, each SBU has its own strategy and operates independently of most other groups within the company. Within General Electric, for example, the Jet Engines Division has little or no connection to the Plastics

Division. For this reason, it is important to understand the strategic direction of each of these divergent SBUs. By understanding the strategies and goals of each SBU, you are then able to develop a plan for helping them achieve their stated goals. Preparing senior executives to visit with a strategic account's executives includes articulating the strategies of each SBU of the account. Your senior executive is then in a position to discuss strategic issues and to help you gain strategic endorsement, or "buy-in," from your customer.

Here is how the process works: You have prepared your senior executive to discuss what you believe is your customer's strategic direction. Your senior executive gains concurrence on these points. (If you are off on a point or two, that is OK; it has probably changed since you gathered the information, anyway.) The job of the senior executive is to clarify the strategy. Once this is done, he is in a position to explain to the customer how your company intends to help it achieve its strategic goals. Here, your executive is seeking confirmation from the customer on what it wants from your company. Once the senior executives of both companies are in agreement, you have top-down buy-in and are very well positioned strategically. This is an envious position.

OPPORTUNITIES FOR SHORT- AND LONG-TERM BUSINESS

You have now had a face-to-face meeting with your key customer executive, and confirmed her strategic direction and the goals and objectives she is targeting. You have obtained buy-in on what your company intends to do to help her achieve her goals.

If you do not have the buy-in at this point, you may be embarking on a very long and very expensive journey to nowhere. How do you get the buy-in from your customer? The simplest way to get strategic buy-in is to ask for it. A common mistake is to see someone you know in the ranks of middle management that you are comfortable with and who will tell you what you want to know. Experience shows, however, that middle managers operate on a tactical level and, while exposed to strategy, they have very little experience in it.

Instead, call the executive vice-president or, if possible, the president. The secretary will probably answer; tell him what you want and ask him to help you. Explain that you are the account executive from your company and that you are responsible for offering your company's resources to his company. Tell him that one of your fundamental steps is to ensure that you are in sync with the strategic direction of his company and that you would like 30 minutes with his boss to confirm that you understand that strategy. And tell him that you would like to show his boss what your company plans to do to help her achieve her strategic goals and to decide which projects you should work on first. This approach is designed to optimize your company's resources and ensures that you are not wasting many people's time in your client's organization.

In some cases, the executive will see you directly; in others, you will need to bring in a person of comparable rank to meet with her. At this level you are dealing with egos, so tread lightly. Once you have met with the senior executive, you are set. You know the strategic direction of the customer and its senior executives have endorsed what your company intends to do. You now have the right to follow up with the senior executive and work with him on an ongoing basis.

The next step is to define several strategic opportunities that will allow you to make a short-term as well as long-term impact. Sales Opportunities, or projects, should be laid out along SBU lines and should contain the following information:

- Project description
- Location
- Our person responsible/phone
- Our technical person responsible/phone
- Sales/service order number
- Proposal/quote number
- Product/service involved
- Projected issues
- Key contacts
- Decision criteria
- Competitors
- Customer perception
- Won/lost; why
- Results
- Dollar value of sales opportunity
- Projected closed date
- Return on investment to the customer/payback period

This may seem like a great deal of information; however, it will allow you to rationally discuss the account possibilities with your senior management. Remember, you are asking them to make a significant investment in your ability to grow the business with this account. You don't have any room for errors at this point. Taking over an account is almost like getting married. You are embarking on an extended relationship, and the relationship has to be managed as a process, not an event. You may not be in total control of your success, but you're certainly accountable, so make sure that you understand the process and how to guide it.

Chapter Six

Presenting the Case to Management

You have spent several weeks or months gathering information on the account and you have been given 10 minutes to present your case to management. What information do you present? Senior executives want to see certain types of information. The following is a presentation a person might make in proposing Boeing as a strategic account. The presentation should be prepared on overheads or other projection method, and a copy of each slide should be given to the managers present. The first slide (figure 6–1), shows basic account information along with the certain financial information. In addition, the AE's name, title, and phone number should also appear.

The next slide (figure 6–2) should be a description of the account's financial picture. From this, your senior executives will make a judgment of the account's stability and long-term growth potential. In the case of Boeing, annual sales are about $20 billion and the annual report shows an order backlog of over $80 billion. This shows long-term stability.

From the financial information, you can determine the potential size of your market. A company will spend a certain percentage of its sales on your particular type of product or service. If you don't know what that percentage

FIGURE 6–1
Basic Information Slide for Boeing

Boeing

7755 East Marginal Way South

Seattle, WA 98252

206-854-9898

Fortune Rank: 16 Industry Rank: 1

Level of Business: $11,565K FYE: Dec. 31

Annual Revenue: $29,200M #Employees: 164,500

---

is, call the customer and ask them how much they spend overall on your type of product or service, and then divide the number by the annual sales to derive a percentage. Comparison of this figure with those of other companies in the same industry will allow you to have some idea of potential market size. For example, in the computer industry, it is fairly well known that a high-tech company will spend from 1 to 2 percent of sales on computer products and services. In engineering services, it is different. Executives look at the annual expense for property, plant, and equipment (PP&E) and make their calculations accordingly. In the case of Boeing, let's assume that 25 percent of PP&E is spent on new facilities or upgrading existing ones. Engineering services fees may then range from 5 to 15 percent of this amount. So if the PP&E for Boeing is

FIGURE 6–2
Financial Information Slide for Boeing

Sales	$20,200B	Assets	$13,278B
Gross profit	1,385	Stockholders' equity	4,452
Net profit	635	Market value	5,587
Long-term debt	275	Stock price	$46.25
		as of	Jan 3, 1991
R&D expense	754	Price/Earnings	11.2
Property, plant, and equipment	1,362	Earnings per share	$4.23
D&B rating	A	% of sales spent on our products	.024%

$1.4 billion, they would spend between $17 million and $51 million on engineering design services for new facilities. This approach can be used to give you an indication of your market potential. It can be calculated from the information in figure 6–2.

You should also be prepared to discuss the availability of funding, the buying cycle, lease vs buy, and any other issues pertinent to the financial condition of the company.

While executives have a propensity for numbers, a graph may tell your story better (see figure 6–3). Most annual reports contain graphics that show five-year histories of key business indicators for the company; you may want to reproduce them as part of your presentation.

During your presentation, you must demonstrate that you understand where your potential strategic account is going in the long term, what its goals and objectives are, and what you are going to do to help them achieve them. Some companies will gladly give you their stated strategy,

FIGURE 6–3
Sample Presentation Graph

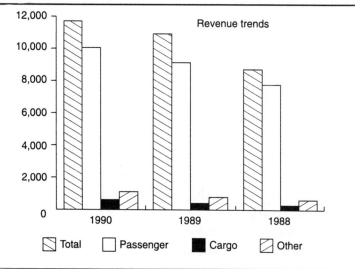

while others guard it very closely. By carefully reading the annual report, you will get a general idea of where the company is headed.

Several years ago, Du Pont published its strategies for each of its business sectors in its annual report. If Du Pont is your strategic account, you are in business. Otherwise, there may be some investigative work to be done. At any rate, once the client's strategies have been discovered, it can be presented in a slide similar to the one shown in figure 6–4. As you might have noted, there is no complementary strategy shown. These strategies will vary based on your business. Some examples are shown in figure 6–5.

These are a few examples to help you create your own complementary strategies. Setting these in place will let your managers know that you are on target, that you un-

FIGURE 6–4
Strategic Positioning for Du Pont Fibers

Du Pont Strategy	Complementary Strategy
Expand new specialty businesses, renew existing products	
Penetrate high-growth areas	

derstand where your customer is going, and that you know how you are going to help its executives achieve their goals. This approach will also serve as a basis for some of your preliminary executive visits. Either you or one of your senior executives can now use this information to obtain strategic buy-in from the customer.

Sit down with the customer executives and confirm that you understand their strategic goals and objectives; then get concurrence from them that the complementary strategies you are proposing are the ones that will help them the most. If there are any differences in opinion, this approach will allow you to make the necessary changes now, not after you have invested a lot of money on the wrong things. The customer will have a tremendous respect for this approach and will be receptive to working with you.

Another part of your presentation to your managers concerns the competitive activity in the account. This involves general statements on your competitors' positions, by division or by SBU. These should describe the products or services and the relationships in place. You may want to add another column to the strategic positioning chart shown in figure 6–4 for comments on competitive activity.

FIGURE 6–5
Examples of Complementary Strategies

Computer Industry Complementary Strategy

Promote the new industrial automation product line to reduce costs and improve efficiency in the existing product lines.

Provide worldwide sales, service, and systems support to all designated areas of market penetration.

Optimize production and distribution costs of high-volume products.

Telecommunications Complementary Strategy

Optimize networking options in new global markets.

Set up telemarketing systems for penetration of high-growth areas.

Use networking to optimize communications for ordering and distribution of high-volume products.

Engineering Design Services Complementary Strategy

Promote our design services for design of new facilities and retro-design of existing manufacturing facilities.

Work with international distribution to design new facility.

Work with corporate engineering to reduce manufacturing costs with new co-gen technology.

The next step is to determine the size of the market. Use the method described earlier to figure the percentage of sales spent on your type of business. This will give you some idea of market size. The approach shown in figure 6–6 will give you an idea of the contract potential for Du Pont's engineering design services.

Once the size of the market is defined, your managers are interested in what your company has done there historically. A five-year sales history by major business segment is necessary and should be presented graphically. Another

FIGURE 6–6
Projected 1994 Contract Potential for
Du Pont

Sales	$37.5B
Total capital spending	$ 5.4B

meaningful measure is the proposal history for the account (see figure 6–7). From this, an idea of percentage wins vs losses can be seen.

The next part of your presentation is an organization chart of the potential client (see figure 6–8). This is more than just a simple organization chart. Make notes for each person represented on the chart, such as Met with, attended seminar, bought previously, Likes us, Likes competition, or Dislikes us.

The next part of your presentation should be five sales opportunities that present the greatest possibility of estab-

FIGURE 6–7
A Sample Proposal History Form

Proposal History						
Date	Division	Project	Our Bid	Win Bid	Competitors	Comments

FIGURE 6–8
A Typical Organization Chart

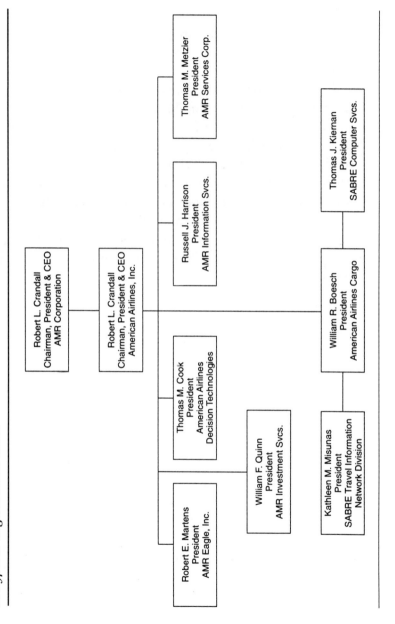

lishing a strategic relationship, if properly managed. Figure 6–9 shows a simple way to present the necessary information.

The final slide in your presentation should show your recommendations. It should include recommended resources, personnel, contracts, discounts, and time frames. It should also include a schedule for account planning sessions and the people who should be involved.

The next move on your part is to ask your managers for the order. If you have done your homework and built your business case, and it indicates that the account should become a strategic account, then it is up to you to ask for the resources you need to effectively grow the account. You deserve it!

FIGURE 6–9
Sample Format for Top Five Sales Opportunities

Description	Location	Key Contact	Phone	Product/ Service	$	% Prob	Net $	Date	Resources	Results
K4N Automation	Wilmington	John Davis	614-321-3144	Design Svcs	$150K	50%	$75K	8-1-93	Technical	TBD
Nylon Refurb	Columbia SC	Bill Heikkila	813-442-1500	Design Svcs	210K	75	$145	9-15-93	Technical	TBD

Chapter Seven

Preparing to Develop the Strategic Account

Now that you have become a strategic account manager, you have a lot of work to do. You have this job because you are good at what you do, but this is new territory with a new set of rules. You have been a tactician and now you are going to have to deal with higher-level executives, some of whom are strategists, some tacticians, and some a combination of both.

BECOME COMFORTABLE CALLING ON TOP EXECUTIVES

Meeting with top client executives is a tall order for some people, but it can be easy for those who know how to get there and what to say once they arrive. Before you call to make the appointment, you need to do your homework. Here are some ideas:

- Set the objective of the call, whether it be positioning, pricing, discovering a sales opportunity, or simply saying thank you for a recent order.
- Ask for the proper amount of time. There are some rules of thumb for how much time to ask for; if you

don't follow them you can look pretty silly and
blow your credibility right at the start.

President or CEO	5 minutes
Executive VP	10 minutes
VP or Division Mgr	15 minutes
Director	30 minutes
2nd-level manager	1 hour
1st-level manager	1/2 day
Technocrat	1 day

• The top-level executives want to know more about
their company, while the lower-level executives
want to know more about your company.
• Top-level executives want to know if you can help
their company. Mid-level executives want to know
how to solve the problem. The technical people
want to know how to implement the solution.

WHAT TO SAY WHEN YOU GET THERE

Be prepared to answer any question you might get from
the executive. Several years ago, I visited a sector vice-
president at General Electric to thank him for the business
he had done with us. As I walked into the office of a man
who managed a $1 billion sector of his company, his first
words were, "How do you guys maintain such a high
P/E ratio?" I was expecting a slightly different reception.
This was his credibility test: Pass it and you're in; fail it
and you're out. To this day I am thankful that I had done
my homework. My response was quick and to the point:
"We are in a group of high-tech blue-chip stocks that have a

higher than normal P/E ratio." Fortunately, that was the right answer. After this encounter, I prepared three sets of questions that have become invaluable to me. You should prepare a set of answers to those asked by top executives and by your managers, as well as a set of questions that you may ask your customer's executives. These questions are designed to give you credibility when you are engaged in a strategic discussion. If these questions are difficult to answer, either research them or ask your senior executives for help. Make certain that your responses are consistent for everyone working with the account.

COMMON QUESTIONS ASKED BY TOP CLIENT EXECUTIVES

1. How do you maintain such a high P/E ratio?
2. How can you continue to grow at greater than 25 percent per year and still finance the growth from internal profits?
3. What are your contributions to introducing new technology?
4. How can you raise your after-tax profits to such a high percentage?
5. What is your DSO (accounts receivable)?
6. How do you minimize your staff's idle time?
7. Are the founders of your company still active?
8. What percent of the stock do your founders own?
9. How would you fare in a takeover bid?
10. Describe the internal philosophy of your company.
11. What is Z Theory?

12. What is your turnover rate?
13. How are you approaching Malcolm Baldrige processes internally?
14. How are you showing Baldrige certification to your customers?
15. Are you requiring your suppliers to be Baldrige-certified?
16. What is your long-term corporate strategy?
17. How have you weathered the current downturn in the economy?
18. How do you involve operational managers with your customers?
19. Where do you get new managers?
20. It seems that you are managing growth; can you explain how?
21. Why don't you sell stock or borrow money to allow faster growth?
22. When do you see your growth leveling off?
23. How can you share technology across all divisions?
24. Do you have an internal information systems council?
25. Where are your profit centers?
26. What is the structure of your sales organization?
27. How does your field organization handle flexible pricing?
28. How do you find and train new people?
29. How do you cope with internal turf issues?
30. Where are you investing in new facilities and acquisitions?
31. Do you own or lease your space?

32. How do you convince your people to travel extensively?

33. Do you have variable pay scales in different parts of the country?

34. How do you handle early retirement?

35. Would you consider setting up electronic billing with us?

36. How do you decide which technology to invest in?

37. How do you ensure that your various divisions do not scatter in all directions with their computer applications?

38. Where do you advertise?

39. Will you advertise on TV?

40. What percentage of your budget do you spend on promotions vs media?

41. Do you use both PCs and Macintoshes on internal projects?

42. How do you manage your communications network?

43. How many government R&D projects do you have?

44. Where do you see your industry in five years?

45. How do you handle strategic planning?

46. What new businesses are you considering going into?

47. What new geographic areas are you exploring?

48. With which companies do you have strategic alliances?

49. Which companies do you own part of?

50. Are you looking to sell off any business segments?

QUESTIONS TO ASK TOP EXECUTIVES, WITH CAUTION

1. What is your position in your industry?
2. How are you weathering the current downturn in the economy?
3. Where do you see the current economy going?
4. How are you preparing to cope with it?
5. At what percentage capacity are you running?
6. What resources, either internal or external, are most critical to your success?
7. How are you currently viewed by Wall Street?
8. What is your corporate mission statement?
9. What are your corporate values?
10. What is your current P/E ratio?
11. What is your growth strategy?
12. Do you view your company as a takeover candidate?
13. How would you battle a takeover bid?
14. Do you have a poison pill in place? If so, please describe it.
15. Are you in an acquisition mode?
16. Where do you see your company in three years?
17. How do you handle strategic planning?
18. How are you organized with respect to profit centers?
19. From which levels of management do you require multiyear plans?
20. Who are your biggest competitors?
21. Are you and your competitors friendly rivals or bitter enemies?

22. How do you fare in the international market?

23. Do you see the Japanese as a major threat?

24. How would you characterize your management style (X, Y, or Z)?

25. How are you handling office automation?

26. How are you handling the deployment of notebook technology?

27. How do you use quality circles?

28. Do you have steering committees at the corporate level or the division level?

29. How are beta tests run in your company?

30. How do you work with local universities in the areas of research and donations?

31. Where do you get your people (e.g., are they experienced or straight from college?)?

32. What outside consulting services do you use?

33. Do you use outside placement firms?

34. Do you outsource any services?

35. Who is your credit firm?

36. How have the recent tax-law changes impacted your business and investments?

37. How do you select your consulting firms?

38. Where do you see technology going in the next five years?

39. How do you plan to integrate new technology into your company?

40. What do you look for in a company such as ours?

41. Do you allow your employees to buy from your corporate purchase agreements?

42. How often and when during the year do you reorganize?

43. When do you do capital budgeting?

44. What is your procedure for getting large capital procurements approved?

45. Are you familiar with our executive seminars?

46. How do you measure productivity?

47. How are you handling the Malcolm Baldrige quality push, both in your organization and with your suppliers?

48. How do you help your customers monitor and increase their productivity and quality?

49. What is your familiarity with our company?

50. Who are the key people in your company we should spend time with to maximize your return?

TYPICAL QUESTIONS ASKED BY YOUR MANAGERS

1. How are we strategically positioned?

2. Who do we know?

3. What have we done with the customer recently?

4. Who is our executive contact person?

5. When did they last attend one of our functions?

6. What was the function?

7. When did they last attend a competitor's function?

8. What was the function?

9. How can we influence the client?

10. Can we leverage our success into new areas?

11. How are we protecting our base business?

12. What are the growth opportunities?

13. What are the new business opportunities?
14. What are the competitive activities?
15. Does the client do quarterly planning with our competitor?
16. Would they be receptive to a quarterly planning approach with us?
17. How is their business?
18. Who are their competitors?
19. What are the competitive trends in their industry?
20. Who are their key customers?
21. What are their market tactics?
22. What are their distribution channels?
23. What are their critical success factors?
24. What is their current financial position?
25. What are their business constraints?
26. How are we impacted by their business constraints?
27. What is our business history with the customer?
28. Where have we made mistakes in the past, and will they impact our future relationship?
29. What relationships do the senior executives or their kin have with our competitors?
30. Are we in a position to hire any of their key people leaving on early retirement?
31. Are we in a position to hire any of the children of their key people?
32. How do their senior executives like to be entertained?
33. What events do they sponsor?
34. What events have they attended that we sponsor?
35. What charities do they sponsor?

36. Which of their senior executives runs the United Way program?
37. What are their internal turf issues?
38. Who are expected to be winners in the long run?
39. What is the impact if we guess wrong?
40. How are we tactically positioned?
41. How long has the opportunity been forecast?
42. When will it close?
43. Are we dealing with the proper people?
44. Do we have the right resources in place?
45. Where are we vulnerable?
46. What are the "gotchas"?
47. Who are we dealing with?
48. How do they make decisions?
49. How well is the decision process working?
50. Can we move up the close date?
51. What have you done for me today?

Some organizations feel that preparing their people to answer these questions is so important that they have produced videotapes with senior executives describing the answers. If you look carefully at the set of questions that your managers are going to ask you, there are only 10 questions that are tactical, or focused on a specific deal. The rest are strategic. Most sales training systems focus on the tactical questions because there are fewer of them and they have positive short-term impact. Without answering the first 40 questions with a solid knowledge of your account, you will have fewer chances to answer the last 10. A person who specializes in one-shot deals concentrates on the last 10 tactical questions; once the deal is closed, they move on to another account because they have no real knowledge of what is going on with this one. In the real world, we would relate them to the person who lives on one-night stands. There are salespeople who are very successful with this approach. They are not the type of people who will do well in managing a strategic account, however, because they do not take the time to build relationships.

Senior executives sometimes make the mistake of thinking that a salesperson who is extremely successful selling in a territory with several hundred accounts will be successful in managing one large account. This is not always true. There is a definite personality difference between the small-business rep and the strategic account rep. One is a mercenary and the other is a general. An even worse scenario occurs when a manager of small-business reps is promoted to manager of strategic account managers; the likely outcome is either mutiny or mass exodus. In short, it is critical to match the personalities and backgrounds of the people to the functions they perform.

While running a computer sales district in Virginia for Hewlett-Packard, my organization was simple. The person selling to the military was a graduate of the Naval Academy; the person selling to the state of Virginia had a degree in political science; individuals selling to manufacturers were industrial engineers; the very technical accounts went to civil and nuclear engineers; and my mercenary was a former college quarterback with an MBA who had an absolute one-night-stand personality. He was excellent at discovering and closing new business but was weak on long-term relationships. We were never under quota and our customer satisfaction ratings were always at the top of the surveys.

Chapter Eight

How Can We Develop the Appropriate Relationships?

Now that you are comfortable with what to say to senior executives, it is time to explore more than just a typical sales call. Having accepted this position, it is expected that you will develop a very strong strategic relationship between the two companies. This type of relationship does not happen overnight; it takes time and typically occurs over several years. The question is, Where do you begin?

Hopefully, during your account investigation phase you developed some inside contacts and have discovered if any of your senior executives have any inside contacts you can leverage. This is the easy way, but we will take it from the start. We know, or think we know, the strategic direction of our client; we have a plan for helping them achieve these goals; we know who the senior executives are; and we have some general idea of what their areas of responsibility are.

I have always found that the direct method is the most effective. Decide which senior executive can help you the most, pick up the phone, and call her. There is a 95 percent chance that you will get her secretary unless you call before 7:45 AM or after 5:15 PM, when the executive will normally answer her own phone. If the secretary answers, explain why you are calling: "Hello, this is Wayne Perry with XYZ Corporation. I am the strategic account executive for your company and I need your help. Our company is focusing significant resources on cultivating the business relationship between our two companies and we would like to meet with Jane [never use Mr. or Ms. unless all you know is the last name] for 10 minutes to verify that we have a handle on your strategy and to confirm that the resources that we are bringing to bear on your company are the right ones and that we are using them in the right places. We do not want to waste your people's or our people's time, and Jane can help us focus our efforts. George Simons, our executive vice-president of operations, would like to accompany me on our meeting, and we would like to schedule 10 minutes either next Thursday or Friday. What time would Jane have open?"

The secretary knows all she needs to know to confirm the meeting: who, what topic, when, where, why, and how long. She will have to confirm this with Jane, but you can ask that she "pencil you in" until the confirmation is made. If you have a credible story, you will get to see Jane.

If you are fortunate enough to have Jane answer her own phone, the conversation will follow the same path: "Hello Jane, this is Wayne Perry. I am the strategic account manager from XYZ Corporation covering your account. We are investing in the business relationship between our two companies and we would like 10 minutes of your time to confirm that we are headed in the right direction. The last thing we want to do is stumble around and waste a lot of your people's time and our people's time. We want to streamline the interaction and only work on those things that will make a difference. George Simons, our executive vice-president of operations, and I would like to confirm several things with you, such as your strategic direction and what we plan to do to help you achieve your strategic objectives. If these need some up-front corrections, we want your input. From here, we would like you to help us focus on where we should apply our resources. It should not take more than 10 minutes; I wonder if we could get together either Tuesday or Wednesday of next week in your office?"

Jane knows exactly what you want and should agree to see you, since you are bringing an executive vice-president with you. There is a risk here in playing an ace on the first round, but the stakes are high. It is not appropriate for Jane to push you down in the organization with this fire-power on your side unless she has no intention of doing business with your company or unless she is going to be out of town.

For your meeting with Jane, you should prepare the same way you did for your briefing to your managers. There is a decision on whether you or your executive vice-president (EVP) is going to carry the meeting. There is a place for both of you and if you handle the shared responsibility, you both win.

First and foremost, this is your account. As you arrive in Jane's office, introduce yourself first and then your EVP. Restate the purpose of the meeting and thank Jane for the appointment. Have your EVP begin the discussion of your commitment to the strategic account program. Explain that you begin your approach by looking at a client's strategic direction and at what your company can do to help them achieve their goals. Once you are in agreement on strategic direction, then you can set a course of action that will optimize the return on your investment and resources.

The next step is for your EVP to present your understanding of Jane's company's strategic goals and objectives and to gain concurrence. Once this step is complete, the EVP should defer the conversation to you. It is your job to explain, point by point, how your company plans to help Jane's company achieve its objectives. There should not be more than five strategic points to discuss. Once these are presented, ask Jane for her buy-in. If she is not satisfied, then ask her to tell you how you can help her and her company. Once you have agreement on strategies, the next step is to ask Jane who the key contacts and projects are. Tell her you don't want to waste anyone's time and you want to work on the projects that make the most sense for both of you.

This is an honest and straightforward approach, and Jane should respect it and provide valuable insight. You might continue the discussion by telling Jane that you would like to follow up with her as the relationship continues to develop and keep her apprised of what is going on. At the same time, your EVP should invite Jane to call on him at any time and let Jane know that he plans to follow up with her personally as well. This will show Jane that this is not just a courtesy call, that there is substance to your visit. Make certain that you and your EVP send Jane a letter thanking her for the visit and confirming the joint strategic buy-in that was agreed upon at the first meeting.

From this point on, you have strategic buy-in. Don't mess it up!

UNDERSTANDING WHERE AND HOW DECISIONS ARE MADE

A number of high-tech industries teach their sales forces to call on top executives because that is where the decisions are made. This approach was successful through most of the 1980s but began to fall apart as technical affluence grew with the advent and spread of the personal computer. In 1985, I approached Brandt Allen, a professor at the Colgate Darden School of Business at the University of Virginia, with an idea. At the time, we at Hewlett-Packard's Virginia sales district were making all the right moves at the top levels of most companies to establish the proper relationships, and we were very solid with the technical people, but we were losing orders. Our discussions led us to a profile of management within an organization. Here are some of our insights:

- There are four types of people in any group: people who are unaware, people who are aware, people who understand, and people who support.

- One group of people worries about whether you can solve my problem, another worries about how to solve the problem, and another worries about how to implement the solution.

- Some people are strategists; some are tacticians; some are a mix.

- Some people deal with issues; some with problems.

- Some people deal with policy; some specify how funds can best be used; some control costs and are task oriented.

- Some people view your products or services as added costs; some view your expertise as contributing to additional profits.

- Some people view you as a vendor; some view you as a partner.
- Some people read the *Wall Street Journal, Forbes,* and *In Search of Excellence;* some read *Business Week* and trade journals; and some read technical publications.
- Some people attend executive seminars; some attend industry seminars; some attend technical seminars.

Somewhere in this was a clue, but it took some time to finally put all the pieces together. What the high-tech industry had been teaching all these years, calling on top executives because that was where the decisions were made, may be flawed. We began to discover the premise that most of the decisions were made by middle managers, with the approval and buy-in of senior executives and concurrence from the technical people that the implementation was feasible. We were now able to characterize three distinct functional levels within an organization (see figure 8–1). This proved to be a very powerful model.

Much money has traditionally been spent on entertaining and building relationships with the senior executives of an organization, while ensuring that technical people were well informed on product functionality and capability. It is believed that if both areas are covered, then you can't lose. This is not always true! There is a group of top-level tacticians and bottom-level strategists who build the business cases for projects, get the funding approved by senior executives, then decide where and how to spend the money.

FIGURE 8–1
The Three Functional Levels of an Organization

	Mkt/Ad	*Thinking*	*Concerns*	*Position*	*Deals With*
Senior executives	*Wall Street Journal* *Forbes* *In Search of Excellence*	Strategists	Can do	Understand	Issues
Middle managers	Trade journals Direct mail	Strategists/Tacticians	How to Profit	Aware	Problems
Technocrats	Technical journals	Pure Tacticians	How to implement Costs and Schedules	Support	Details

MARKETING TO
MIDDLE MANAGEMENT

The profile of a middle manager is a person who makes top-level tactical decisions and bottom-level strategic decisions. They read such publications as *Business Week* and various trade journals. They are interested in how to implement a project. Typically, they are handed the problems of senior executives and are very aware of what is going on among all competitors.

To build relationships with people at this level, a salesperson must cater to their specific needs. Most people at this organizational level receive compensation based on performance. How can you help them improve their performance while improving your own? One of the most cost-effective ways to build relationships and credibility with middle managers is to educate them. You want to be viewed as an extension of their organization because if they believe you have expertise that they need to improve their position within their organization, you will become invaluable to them. One of the best approaches to the education process is the seminar. One downfall of a lot of companies is using educational seminars as a platform for selling products or services. If it is an educational seminar, stick to education. If it is a product or service promotion, let the attendees know in advance what they are in for. In either case, seminars can be powerful in building relationships.

Now that we had the model in place, it was time to test it out. We knew that a number of companies were very successful at calling on top executives and then following up these efforts with strong ties to the technical community. They sold to the strategists who understood what was going on and to the pure tacticians who were the detailed implementors. Our observation was that they completely missed the middle ground: the people who were charged with making things happen.

Targeting this segment meant changing the way we did business at Hewlett-Packard, but we decided to experiment with the approach of involving middle management in the process. The most cost-effective approach was to conduct a series of educational seminars aimed at the people who were worried about how to solve real-world problems. The seminar concept was not new to the sales process, but we added a few twists. We first investigated how IBM conducted its executive seminar programs. IBM was the acknowledged leader in executive seminars. After careful analysis, we found that, for the most part, IBM's approach was two-tiered. One level addressed senior executives, while the other addressed the technical people. We began to question our wisdom of opening up a whole new area of attack if the industry leaders did not address it. Our background had taught us that the way to succeed in many cases was to change the rules of the game. So the experiment began.

The Seminar Experiment

We clearly understood how to put on a successful senior executive seminar; we had over 20 years of experience in technical seminar programs; but we had no experience in dealing with middle-management seminars. To be considered successful, we had to benefit financially from the effort. We knew from experience that from each person who attended a technical seminar, $2,000 to $5,000 in incremental revenue was achieved. The revenue was traced over a one-year period from the date of the seminar. We were also able to trace that each attendee at an executive seminar produced an average of $100,000 of incremental revenue. Our goal was to get $50,000 in incremental revenue from each attendee at our middle-management program.

We first designed the overall program, setting a framework for the program that included six speakers (four internal and two experts). We had a program moderator, who usually participated in the program as well. Speakers were selected based on their speaking talent and not on their rank in the company. It is very important that you not allow people on the program just because of their rank. A poor speaker will kill you! Sometimes you stake your career on your selection of speakers, but it is your decision. The four internal speakers spoke on general topics such as communications and office automation, while the experts tailored the program to a specific middle-management audience. For example, John White of Systecon, Inc., who was also the director of the Materials Handling Institute at Georgia Tech, spoke on materials handling issues at our manufacturing seminar. Brandt Allen, the noted author with whom I brainstormed the middle-management idea, spoke about setting up information services as a profit center. Phil Jacobs, now the vice-president of national accounts at BellSouth, spoke about linking multilocation organizations with voice and data.

The target audience was the top-level tactician or bottom-level strategist for each of the chosen areas. We wanted two people from each company. To add validity to the invitation process, we would only allow invitations to be delivered by our first-level sales managers, who would also accompany the customers to the seminar. To ensure that this did not become an overbearing sales situation, the sales rep was not included. This created a lot of strife with the sales force but a tremendous amount of credibility with the customers. It presented a great networking opportunity for both our customers and our managers. Each seminar cost about $10,000. The customer was expected to pick up his own travel expenses for the one-day program. Speakers were on for 40 minutes and there was a 20-minute break between each one. Lunch was on us, and this was when a lot of the interaction occurred.

Measuring Success

A set of criteria was established for measuring the return on our investment. We tracked 266 attendees from 66 companies for a period of one year after the seminar. If they got a new idea that resulted in a new project as a result of the seminar, we counted the order at 100 percent value. If they changed vendors on a proposed project and bought from us as a result of what they learned in the seminar, we counted 50 percent of the value of the order. If the seminar stimulated the early release of a purchase order on a project, we counted 25 percent of the order. So there was a devaluing effect on the incremental revenue we counted. We went directly to the sales managers and the customers to verify our findings. After everything was tallied, we found that we were receiving incremental revenue in excess of $100,000 for every middle manager who attended the program. At an average of 30 attendees per seminar and a cost of about $10,000, we were far ahead of our expectations.

What We Learned

All was not perfect with the new middle-management program. Our sales managers were now required to call on higher-level executives in the organization in order to deliver invitations to the seminars. The managers were trained as tacticians and to meet monthly quotas. The people they were talking to now had a different set of issues to discuss. They wanted to discuss profit, productivity, and process. Our managers were not equipped to handle this. Although they had been trained in the major account process and had worked with a set of questions similar to the ones described in chapter 7, they were still not comfortable with how strategists thought or how to talk to them.

I went back to my friend Brandt Allen and explained my new problem. Our original work was on target, but my sales managers were not equipped to carry out the mission. By this time Brandt was working in the Executive Program at the School of Business and we discussed the possibility of sending Hewlett-Packard (HP) managers to one of those sessions. But none seemed to fit our exact needs. Brandt suggested that we do a customized program, based on Harvard case studies, to immerse our managers in the mind-set of the strategist. So we designed a program tailored exactly to what our managers needed to become more comfortable in talking with strategists.

The first program was put on some four months later at the Boar's Head Inn in Charlottesville, Virginia. There were three cases to prepare for each night. This would not be party time; it was serious business and as such the HP managers were very focused. When the program was over, we received comments like this one: "This was great, but

I'm not sure how I can use it." This made us doubt whether we would repeat this program. At the end of two months the attendees were polled again, and the comments were more on the order of: "I now understand the problems my customer's managers face, and we are able to tailor our solutions to meet their business needs and not just the technical needs." The program was adopted for every sales manager and account executive in the company. This added the missing ingredient, and we overcame the language and credibility barriers with middle management.

Middle-management seminars can be run for an individual company or in a geographical area. Chapter 13 is dedicated to conducting executive seminars.

Chapter Nine

Heirs to the Glass Tower

Gaining control of an account may take years of careful planning and execution and a lot of luck. Working with operations people in a client organization and not with the purchasing group is a new adventure for some salespeople and a very calculated departure for others. Purchasing people typically view vendors as a cost and their job is to reduce costs. Operations people are interested in manufacturing at a lower cost per unit, or delivering a new product to market sooner, or driving up the revenue curve with more sales. Executives talk in terms of earnings per share. A long-term approach to gaining control of an account is to begin working with the operations people; as they are promoted to the executive suite, the relationship continues. The following case relates to IBM and how they effectively "owned" accounts and the strategies their top competitors employed to wrestle away that control. This strategy can be used in other industries as well.

In the world of high technology, it goes without saying that for many years *account control* and *IBM* were synonymous terms. Simply put, IBM was awesome. IBM owned the "glass tower," and the executives who lived there listened to and planned with IBM on a regular basis. The people at IBM had excellent relationships with the senior executives in the client organizations and maintained these ongoing relationships by focusing efforts on the higher functional levels in the organization.

A favorite strategy was to begin building the relationship at IBM's Executive Education Programs at Boca Raton, Florida. IBM offered various programs covering a wide range of topics that their best customers gladly attended. The most important aspect of these programs was relationship building, and it really worked. As late as the mid-80s, IBM still owned more than 75 percent of the computer mainframe market, and they catered to those who paid the bills.

IBM's other focal point was at the technical level. Realistically, at that point in time IBM salespeople had all the bases covered. They were protecting their relationships in the executive suite and they controlled the technical people in management information systems (MIS) with their constant technical barrage of new products and services.

The market began to change in the mid- to late 80s with the introduction of what was then known as "distributed processing" and "open systems." Today, these terms are more commonly known as "LAN/WAN applications" and "clones." The market for computer hardware has completely changed and continues to look more and more like the automobile market. The technical knowledge base has moved from MIS out to the users. For some time MIS attempted to control the purchases of all computer technology. But as the prices began to dip below the financial approval level of operations managers, the wishes and backlogs of MIS were ignored and the users were empowered to solve their own business problems without MIS involvement.

As MIS control of applications became distributed across the operational units, IBM's control of the accounts began to falter, even though the relationships at the corporate level were still pretty much intact. IBM's area of dominance in a typical client organization continued to be in the glass tower and MIS (see figure 9–1).

To begin to unravel IBM's dominance in the accounts, competitors started looking at relationships. The question was, How long had it been since these people have graduated from college? Figure 9–2 diagrams the answer.

Typically, the senior executives had been out of school for more than 20 years and the technical people had been out of school for less than 10 years. IBM focused its efforts in the over-20-year and the less-than-10-year segments. This focus was quite acceptable during the mainframe computer era. When the shift to computer purchasing at the departmental level occurred, however, there was a new class of decision makers. They were mid-level managers

FIGURE 9–1
Areas of IBM Influence

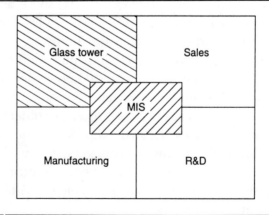

FIGURE 9–2
*IBM's Relationships with Customers, by Number of Years
Since College Graduation*

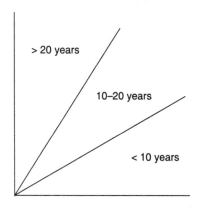

who had been out of school for 10 to 20 years. They were
the leading-edge baby boomers.

The notion of consultative selling was also coming of
age, and for years IBM had done an excellent job of consulting with customers about their business information
needs. But the existing relationships became a double-
edged sword for IBM salespeople. They desperately
needed to establish relationships in the user departments,
but when they attempted to do so, MIS lost control. To
retaliate for IBM's moves to establish these new relationships, MIS would purchase another vendor's mainframe
(thus, the establishment of Amdahl in the marketplace).
To combat this trend, IBM gave birth to its General Systems
Division that sold mid-range systems and turned them
loose at the departmental level. Digital Equipment Corporation (DEC) was already well established in the end user
community with its VAX line and was catering largely to

the manufacturing and R&D side. Hewlett-Packard (HP) was well established in test and measurement equipment, and NCR was very well positioned in the back office of many financial institutions. HP, DEC, and NCR had spent years cultivating relationships at the operational level. They could speak with these people about their business issues and were viewed as technical experts.

The IBM philosophy was to put very smart people from various backgrounds into sales and train them in systems, applications, and industry specifics. This was a solid plan in the mainframe world, but once in the operations areas of the business, salespeople were expected to know the operations side of the business cold. HP, DEC, and NCR took advantage of the shift to distributed systems as well as IBM's new openness by placing salespeople with engineering backgrounds with client engineers in R&D and manufacturing, and salespeople with operations experience in finance with operations people in financial institutions.

With the threat of antitrust actions and a possible breakup of IBM, the company became very open when it came to information on its product and service offerings. Ordering a catalog of IBM's product literature and manuals was as easy as a phone call to the local office. From this catalog, virtually any IBM publication could be ordered. So when competitors engaged IBM, they would order a full set of literature and sample boilerplate proposals from this catalog. This was a glaring hole in IBM's information distribution system. When you have a competitor's full set of literature and a copy of the proposal the customer is going to get, you can plan a fairly effective strategy to counter its every move.

In addition to emulating IBM's Executive Education Programs, competitors began to focus on a series of middle-management seminars geared to the heirs of the glass tower. These relationships were strong and lasting because the heirs felt that HP, DEC, and NCR helped educate and consult with them and did not necessarily try to sell to them. HP, DEC, and NCR also spent time educating their sales forces on how to work closely with senior executives. Major account, national account, and global account programs were born. These companies brought in knowledgeable people in the functional and operational areas of multiple industries and funneled them into specific account niches. They then educated them on the strategic processes such as account and relationship management. For example, a typical rep calling on a manufacturing division of General Electric was an industrial engineer with a 3.0 GPA or higher, with 3 to 5 years of industry experience and APICS (American Production and Inventory Control Society) certified. A rep calling on state government majored in political science at the local state university. Operational skills were carefully matched to customer type.

IBM found its relationships at the executive level diminished, mainly because of senior executive retirements. The fallback position was to rely on the technical relationships in MIS. IBM began to find that the competitors' relationships at the top were in some cases better because the competitors had nurtured relationships early on with the heirs to the glass tower.

Chapter Ten

The Account as a Market—Finding the Sales Opportunity

Classical market segmentation deals with an aggregate of customers located in a general geographic area or with a vertical market segment. This is a great approach from the perspective of the MBAs in the corporate ivory tower who set global corporate strategy, but what about the poor guy in the trenches who is trying to interpret this strategy and put it into some type of tactical game plan to meet a quota?

The account executive is in all probability not that concerned with what the corporate marketing staff is doing on a day-to-day basis. He is concerned about his customers and how he can best serve their needs. He is also concerned about how he is going to grow the business with a finite number of accounts year after year.

The sales manager is even more perplexed when he is managing a multifaceted sales organization that may have more than one sales rep selling different product lines to the same account. The manager begins to ask himself questions about cross-training sales reps, getting greater productivity by leveraging products and knowledge of the customer, and so on. But until now there have been very few effective tools to allow the sales manager and the account executive to do their jobs and still provide the corporate marketing staff a feedback mechanism on market activity.

Our goal, therefore, will be to examine the problem of proper market segmentation and resource allocation on a micro, or customer-by-customer, level.

We can view a customer (or, more importantly, a company or a division location) as an island in the middle of the ocean. The island requires raw materials to be brought in from the outside supply lines, and some type of defense. The client company has a central core supported by a communications network, which in turn is tied to various functions of the organization. Supporting these functions are the individual operations of the company. In classical military terms, the customer is an island that you are trying to attack. Taking the island gains you the client's order and its continuing business. The defenses you are facing are your competitors as well as the political climate and financial position of your customer. It is up to you to find the appropriate points of attack that will minimize your losses and maximize your gains.

There is nothing new about this military approach, but by looking at a company as an island (in a sales or marketing sense), you are now able to begin a dissection process. You see the core of the company and its surrounding operations, as shown in figure 10–1.

A model of this type will allow us to logically expand our thinking into new areas. The functions shown below the horizontal line are generic and will appear, for the most part, in all companies, regardless of their type of business. It is those operations above the horizontal line that begin to describe specific industry types. It becomes relatively simple to adapt the model to manufacturing, government

FIGURE 10–1
A Manufacturing Customer Dissected by Function

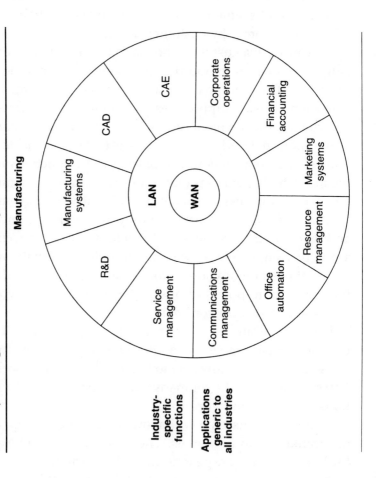

contractors, the distribution industry, or the financial industry merely by altering the functional areas that support the core of the company.

It is at this point that we begin to look at which applications are needed to support the particular operation or function of the organization. These application areas may vary as industry types become more and more specific and as room is allocated in the model to allow for them. Customize the manufacturing model to the electronics industry or the textiles industry simply by adding a few operations specific to those industries and by inserting the applications that support the operations. Figure 10–2 shows that distribution companies can also be modeled.

BUILDING THE MODEL

We should probably begin by agreeing on which functions or operations are in our generic manufacturing company. Even more important is the agreement on which operations are generic enough to be included in all companies. Those which seem to continually appear include:

- Corporate operations
- Marketing systems
- Human resource management
- Communications management
- Office automation
- Financial accounting

Our generic manufacturing organization will add the following functional areas:

- Research and development (R&D)
- Computer-aided design (CAD)

FIGURE 10–2
The Generic Model Adapted to a Distribution Company

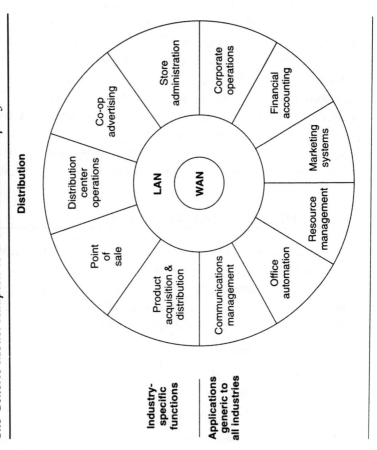

Distribution

Industry-
specific
functions

Applications
generic to
all industries

Store administration
Co-op advertising
Distribution center operations
Point of sale
Product acquisition & distribution
Communications management
Office automation
Resource management
Marketing systems
Financial accounting
Corporate operations

LAN

WAN

- Computer-aided engineering (CAE)
- Manufacturing systems
- Service management

Still pretty simple, right? By laying out the operations that support these functional areas, along with the appropriate applications, we begin to see a good generic model of the organization.

Models are great, but what do we do with them? First we focus on intelligence information. Before any general musters forces to fight an enemy, he must know what his objectives are and as much information as possible about his enemy. He knows that frontal assaults on enemy positions of strength are fatal in 99 percent of the battles fought in history. The same is true in our case. We must characterize our competitor's position and avoid frontal assaults. Our position should also not be one of simply lobbing mortar shells, in the form of literature and random phone calls, into the client company just to keep the customer aware of our presence. If you are the customer, you may find incoming mortar shells a real nuisance, particularly if there is no real battle. In short, we must gather pertinent information on the customer and our competitors from as many sources as is reasonable. To determine what is reasonable, ask yourself the question, "Does my competitor know more about this particular situation than I do?" If the answer is yes, you are in trouble already. Five questions will elicit essential information on each application or operational area:

1. *Who* (which competitor, including corporate MIS) owns this area?
2. *When* was the application installed? When are new

projects scheduled for implementation in this area? When will the current application be replaced?

3. *How much* was spent on the application (e.g., for hardware, software, and support)?

4. How does the operation or application *communicate* with the rest of the organization?

5. Who is the *manager* responsible for the operation or application, and what is the manager's phone number?

Now we're getting somewhere. The outer perimeter of the island is now being determined. Depending on the product line you are responsible for, the data gathering may take only a few minutes, or it could take up to a year to do it completely. The data are broken down into logical segments so we can "divide and conquer." Each sales rep can gather data in his own area of responsibility in the account. The information is then compiled in one place as part of the overall account plan.

At the beginning of a battle, we are working with sketchy intelligence data, but we need to know what type of resources we have at our disposal. With the next layer of the model, we begin to develop our plan of attack. Here we can identify all of the resources we can allocate, in the form of applications expertise, hardware, software, and so on, to a specific operational area of the client organization. Both internal and systems-integration solutions should be identified.

Figure 10–3 shows similar information shown in figure 10–1, but in spreadsheet form. A database can be built using a spreadsheet program to keep track of this type of information.

FIGURE 10–3
The Generic Manufacturing Model in Spreadsheet Form

					3rd Party	Competitive
Organization	SIC Code					
Division	# EMP					
Function	Return on Assets					
					3rd Party	Competitive
Operation/Application	Manager Responsible		Value	When	Solutions	Offerings
Materials Management						
Production Management						
Labor Analysis						
Incoming Inspection						
Vendor History						
Manufacturing Test						
Distributed NC						
Material Handling						
ASRS						
Facilities Layout						
Purchasing						

BECOMING A GENERAL

Generals become generals by effectively leading troops at
the enemy's point of weakness. It is essential not to waste
precious resources by attacking a competitor's position of

strength. Why attack a fortress when you can surround it and cut off its supplies and resources? In our case, why make a frontal assault on a competitor's stronghold when you can provide greater value in another area of the operation and effectively cut off the funding for the competitor's products and services. In a real-world case, let's assume your customer has standardized on Sun Microsystems workstations for computer-aided engineering (CAE). Your probability of success in attacking Sun head-on is very, very low if you are trying to outperform Sun in this environment. Step back from the problem and decide what you have a chance of selling. First, only about 15–20 percent of an engineer's time is spent actually doing CAE. About 10 percent is spent in the test phase of product development, but about 70 percent is spent communicating ideas, either orally or in writing, throughout his organization. So, can you provide the best system for communicating engineering ideas throughout the organization and still provide a satisfactory engineering workstation? Here is a potential point of vulnerability; take advantage of it. Focus your resources on the point of vulnerability and strive for penetration. Take advantage of the strengths of your product line and services and your superior knowledge of this niche operation. Once you have made a penetration into the account, then move from a position of strength, capitalizing on this position in new areas of opportunity.

Companies have a tendency to abandon a position of strength in order to attack a competitor's stronghold, with the goal of expanding sales. If the move is not carefully planned and you do not have a firm plan to protect your incumbent position, there is typically a loss on both fronts. The model should help avoid these pitfalls by giving a graphical view of both your position and that of your competitors.

The next concern in a battle is determining what the enemy is up to. What forces are your competitors going to bring against you when you make your move? The next layer of the model allows us to see what the competitors can offer in the operational or application area. With this information, we can plan a counterstrategy or contingency plan well in advance of the actual encounter. Lieutenants typically have a single-level contingency plan established for every action. Generals always have a contingency plan or at least two alternate courses of action well planned in advance.

We have not yet discussed anything profound, but have only simplified the complex. Now we can see all aspects of an organization and where we stand in relation to our competitors and to our customer, all on one piece of paper. Ultimately, there should be a separate model completed for each division of your customer's organization. It is also critical, when dealing with a remote division, to note which operational areas or applications are handled centrally by corporate headquarters.

Once completed, this model becomes a tool for the front-line troops. Deployment of critical resources is the prime responsibility of the local manager. Knowing how many support troops to call in and when to call them are equally critical. Global marketing decisions can also be made using the gathered data. With a small amount of additional information, we can create a comparative model of companies in similar industries.

If we know the level of expenditures on each application or operational area, the number of employees at the location, and the return on assets for the division, we can begin to compare several companies in similar industries and begin to consult on the spending patterns and priorities of the most profitable organizations.

THE ACCOUNT AS A MARKET— THE IMPLEMENTATION

When looking at an account, there are many aspects that need to be addressed in a logical manner. First, identify the organization you want to attack. This is nothing more than the name of the company, division, department, and the like. Next, discover the functional areas of the organization. This may be finance, manufacturing, communications, or other operations. The size of the organization will determine the complexity of the functional support areas. The individuals who head these areas are typically the most influential in the decision-making process for purchasing goods and services. Of course, board of directors' approval is required in many cases when the level of expenditure is high. This is especially common for nonbudgeted items.

Each of these functional areas is supported by various operations. For example, the financial function is supported by the accounts payable department, the accounts receivables department, and the financial analysis group, among others. The operations areas are in turn supported by various computer applications. We have been on a quest for organizational understanding, but now our skills come into play by having to fit our solution offerings into the operational areas. This is usually our downfall because we have a tendency to jump straight to solution offerings before we find out what the customer is trying to do and even before we assess our own probability of success.

Prior to investing a lot of time and energy, it would be nice to know who, in a competitive sense, may already be performing the particular application we are interested in. Next, when was the application installed or last overhauled? Who is the manager in charge of the operation, and did they make the original purchase decision? How much money was spent on hardware, software, and support services? How does the operation or application communicate with the rest of the organization? A great deal of additional data is obviously needed to sell to a particular application area, but these types of questions will provide a clear indication of whether or not we should expend resources in a particular area.

For example, if your mission is to sell office automation to a particular account and you find that the central organization has a large IBM mainframe supported by a distributed network of AS/400s in an X.25 network, running PROFS on IBM PCs, then it becomes questionable as to whether a frontal assault on this stronghold makes sense. We may see however, that a flanking attack on the desktop publishing area may be our best chance for penetration.

When the salespeople begin to plan strategy, two other pieces of information are essential. First, they should know all of their own internal solutions and the third-party solutions available in these application areas. Second, a brief rundown of the competitor's offerings is also critical in the planning process.

The micro-market segmentation model (see figure 10–1) will now allow you to put all of the account information on one piece of paper. Each operation, however, is analyzed one at a time and then pieced together to form an entire picture of the account. On a large account, it may take up to a year to compile all of the information, and the sales rep should not be expected to gather it all over a weekend. It should also be noted that a separate model is required for each division of an account. The only variation will be in the operation and application data. Another advantage of the micro-market segmentation model is that we can now determine our strategic sales opportunity and map our resources accordingly.

In summary, we have looked at an account in all of its generic parts: organization, function, operation, application, internal and third-party solutions, competitive offerings, and opportunity data. The one area omitted is the internal politics of the organization. This is critical to your success and something only the account executive can handle successfully.

The level of acceptance of this approach will vary. Senior account executives will believe that they already have all of this information in their heads. Many of them do have a great deal of information, but the beauty of the model comes into play when there is a new member of the team, when there is a new management assignment, or when you are attempting to allocate global resources to the account. It all falls into place when you realize, for instance, that Exxon buys more computers than all of the companies in the state of Vermont combined. Thus, Exxon must be approached in the same way as all of those companies in Vermont. Both are markets; one is geographic, and the other is an organization.

Chapter Eleven

The Account Planning Process

The *account planning process* is broken into five distinct areas: strategic mapping, relationship management, opportunity management, resource management, and tactical planning.

Strategic account planning focuses on the long-term aspects of the relationship between two organizations. It serves as a guideline for charting a course of action. The *tactical account plan* provides short-term direction, bringing together marketing strategy, budgets, and tactics. (See figure 11–1.)

STRATEGIC ACCOUNT PLANNING

Effective strategic account planning provides an account sales team and the customer with an accurate picture of what will happen in the relationship, the resources to be committed by both parties, and the expected results. It is important to internalize the fact that account planning is not an event, but an ongoing process. Account planning provides a number of benefits:

- Involves management at all levels.
- Defines direction with specific desired results and time frames.

FIGURE 11–1
A Comparison of Strategic and Tactical Account Plans

Strategic Account Plan	Tactical Account Plan
Time frame—>1 Year	Time frame—<1 Year
Focuses on Top Management	Focuses on Mid-Management
Long-term goals & objectives	Short-term operational strategy/ tactics
Allocation of resources by major SBUs	Estimate of sales revenues and expenses for operational units.

- Allocates resources objectively.
- Provides a common information base for all participants.
- Clarifies the roles and responsibilities of account team members.
- Enhances communications, both internally and externally.
- Keeps remote sites informed.
- Involves the right people.
- Allows multilevel contingency plans to be developed.

The strategic account plan requires periodic updates in response to dynamic events. The key phase is the implementation. Management sometimes overlooks this element. A strategic account plan may be developed and then put in a drawer until the next year, when it must be updated. If this is your approach, then developing the plan in the first place will be a waste of time.

The most successful strategic account plans allow customer involvement. Some sales managers and top executives balk at this notion. They believe that they know what the customer wants and that it is up to the sales force to go and sell it. This is incredibly shortsighted and will ultimately lead to their demise. Those companies that involve their customers in the planning process will ultimately be the most successful. They know what the customer wants to buy and how they want to buy it. The discussion can then shift toward delivery and implementation and away from the selling process.

The account planning process will vary among organizations. Some will take a very structured approach, and others will take a somewhat loose approach, following general guidelines. As the process moves from strategic to tactical, the participants will become more comfortable.

Developing the strategic account plan is a demanding task that requires an understanding of your customer from a strategic perspective. The strategic account plan should dovetail with your customer's strategy. The next step is developing the tactical account plan.

The account planning process provides a means to an end. While developing the initial strategic account plan is difficult, developing the tactical account plan can be an equally daunting task. The first planning session for any account is absolutely the worst yet most necessary thing you must go through. The meeting generally begins with a group of people, all of whom have information on the specific account in question. Everyone wants to talk about the great things they have done for the account. This process is interesting and necessary, but from a planning standpoint it does not accomplish much for the first several hours. Toward the end of the session, all of the background information is on the table, and then the planning can begin. There are a number of problems that can crop up during the planning phase:

- Information is imperfect and incomplete. Plans must be made with the best available information, considering cost and resource constraints.
- Never try to predict anything, especially the future. Errors will occur while forecasting growth opportunities, expenses, and sales.
- The people involved may not be planners and may be unprepared.
- Personality conflicts or hidden agendas may interfere.
- There may be too many attendees.
- Some people may want to avoid responsibility.
- There may be a lack of commitment by top and middle management. This makes the exercise quite futile.
- Balance the time and resources it takes to plan an account with the expected return.
- Balance creativity with what can be accomplished over a finite time frame.
- There may be conflict between strategic and operational decisions. Can you meet quotas while developing the account?

TACTICAL ACCOUNT PLANNING

The tactical account plan generally has a time frame of less than one year, is developed by middle management, is concerned with operational strategy and tactics, and has specific sales revenue and resource requirement forecasts.

Our approach to tactical account planning focuses on a six-month planning window that is updated every 90 days. This becomes known as the rolling six-month plan. The formality of the process will vary from organization to organization, but the basics are the same. Objectives, targets, action items, and performance measures will be set; detailed implementation plans will be put in place. Implementation will be reviewed and corrective actions made. The results will be significant breakthroughs in performance.

Chapter Twelve

The Account Planning Session

"Why should I worry about account planning? I'm always over quota" is the cry of the sales rep who will probably always be a sales rep. The old adage of "plan your work and work your plan" is no truer than in account management. There are always more than just one sales rep involved in a large, complex account sales situation. Everyone must be involved in the planning process so they know what is going on and so all activities can be coordinated among all the groups represented.

The first meeting held to discuss account planning is normally a preplanning meeting. It is held to discuss who should attend the formal planning session, where it will be held, and its duration and agenda. The preplanning session is imperative; assignments should come from this meeting and should be distributed to all participants of the formal planning session. The preplanning session should last one to three hours, depending on the complexity of the account, and should be free of phone interruptions.

One person should be selected to facilitate the formal planning meeting and be responsible for objectively leading the planning process. The facilitator will guide the planning process and ensure that schedules are met and that the appropriate information is distributed to the appropriate participants. It is best to use a facilitator who has no vested interest in the account. Some consultants will also lead account planning sessions. This approach might work since consultants are not constrained or impacted politically by the questions they might ask.

Here are some important points you will want to cover during the preplanning session:

- The strategic account management process.
- The final product (the strategic account plan).
- Information the salespeople feel will be important to their success and how to get it.
- Sources of information within the client organization.
- Assignment of action items to get the required information. Try to limit the time required for this task to under one-half day and remember that meeting quota is the primary objective. What we are asking for is a process that will allow quota to be met more easily.
- Schedule for the actual account planning session, which should be held two to three weeks in the future.

Information should be presented in written form, with copies for everyone on the team. The information should also be distributed on disk, in a common format, to all participants. To avoid having to combine data from all members of the account team, you could use a software program designed specifically for managing large accounts and have everyone on the account team input the data to one common database.

Success in any planning process, especially involving a new concept, requires executive commitment and continuous follow-up. This is a team effort and all members must contribute to the overall success.

The facilitator for the formal planning session should attend the preplanning session and be responsible for tracking the progress of the information gathering. It is imperative that everyone attend the account planning session with the appropriate information.

THE LOGISTICS OF AN ACCOUNT PLANNING SESSION

Schedule the account planning session at an off-site location for one to two days. Schedule breaks every three hours. One option is to schedule work sessions for 8:30–12:00 and 1:00–4:00, a break at 4:00–6:00, dinner at 6:00–7:00 and a work session for 7:00–10:00. This arrangement provides time for small groups to meet and make key decisions that can contribute to the overall plan.

A planning session is most successful if you work through each section on the agenda very methodically, one section at a time, documenting as you go. Then each section is collected and assembled into a draft of the plan.

Who to Invite

It is difficult to decide who should attend the preplanning session while the account team is being formed. Expense is also an issue. If you are selling to General Electric (GE) worldwide, the preplanning session would not include everyone who sells to GE. A more logical approach is to invite the person designated as the GE account executive, plus executives from the top five revenue-producing locations. The vice-president of your national accounts division should also be present and may serve as facilitator. One or two technical managers, if appropriate, should also be present. Once the account team is in place, the attendees to the account planning sessions will always be the account team. The one variable that we have not discussed is the customer.

Many sales managers do not want to involve the customer at all in the account planning process. If this is the case, why are we going through the process of planning our account activities in the first place? The idea is to maximize the return on the resources we are deploying in the account. If we are directing our resources to the wrong places, we are wasting significant time and money. But if you involve the customer in your planning process, you will succeed because the customer has the same motives you do. He does not want to waste time or money. If you are sending your staff to work with his staff on the wrong things, you are wasting his staff's time. Ask the customer to help you decide where to put your finite resources so they will bring the most benefit to him. If he is not interested in helping you in this process, you either have the wrong person, or you have the wrong account.

The individual from the customer's organization should be at a level high enough to provide a proper perspective to what you are trying to accomplish and should be involved in and understand the planning process. These are normally middle managers who are concerned with "how to" solve problems. They will not get bogged down in the details of implementation but will steer you to the appropriate people in their organization. It is normally easier to get a "technical friend" to help in the planning process, but this is a mistake in most cases. They are too low in the customer's hierarchy to have the necessary perspective, and they normally have pet projects they want done. Many organizations have staff planning groups that can be of great assistance in account planning sessions. These groups have a great deal of clout in their organization, so this relationship should be cultivated. Although these staff planning people rarely make decisions for purchases, they can become great allies.

Notification of Participants

The facilitator will personally be responsible for notifying the selected attendees in writing at least two weeks prior to the account planning session. The letter will state information about the planning session, the participants, and their responsibilities.

If this is a new account in the strategic account program and this is the preplanning session, it is important that all participants understand their roles and responsibility in the overall process. Be specific in what is expected of the participants. The following memo can serve as a guide:

(Date)

(List of attendees)

Subject: Account planning session for (account name)

On (date), there will be an account planning session for (account name) at the (location) beginning at (time).

    During this session, we will lay the groundwork for the (account name) account plan. We will determine where we are now, where we need to go, and how we intend to get there. Please bring your account information and be prepared to discuss it in detail. You should be prepared to spend 15 minutes discussing the current situation in the account from your perspective, the key people and their roles, the customer's strategic direction, what we can do to help them reach these objectives, and the short- and long-term business opportunities.

Bring a copy of all presentation materials for each attendee listed above. Be prepared to spend the entire day, free of interruptions, focused on (account name). Here are some simple ground rules we will follow:

- One idea will be discussed at a time.
- One conversation will be held at a time.
- Every issue will be resolved with a definite yes or no (no maybes).
- Every issue will be faced and resolved.
- Votes will be taken to gain consensus. Only two types of disagreement are allowed; basic issues and wording.
- Everyone must participate as peers, each with an equal vote. Each participant should feel free to contribute to the ideas presented.
- There are no bad ideas. No idea will be immediately discarded just because several participants do not agree. It will instead become one of the ideas that will be prioritized at the end of the planning session.
- At the end of the session, a six-month rolling plan will be put in place, with specific activities and due dates assigned. This plan will be updated every 90 days for the next six months.

- If there are any sensitive issues or if the discussion is inhibited on an issue, anyone may be dismissed, including the facilitator.

We are expecting your active participation and look forward to your contributions. See you on (date).

Regards,

(Your name)

LET THE PLANNING SESSION BEGIN

The facilitator is in charge and drives the process. The planning session should begin by stating the situational background and the objectives for the day. A brief discussion of the agenda, breaks, facilities, and expectations is appropriate. The roles and responsibilities of each participant are spelled out as well. The role of the facilitator is to guide the participants and make sure the ground rules and agendas are followed. The role of the participants is to plan and to evaluate the results. It is the mutual responsibility of all participants to work toward stated objectives. In the intensity of a session of this type, maximum effectiveness is achieved if there is a 10-minute break every hour. Attendees are expected to participate fully and to return promptly after breaks. Telephone interruptions are unacceptable; arrangements should have been made in advance to intercept and handle phone calls.

The purpose of the session is to develop a preliminary action plan for the account and to enhance participation in the process through communication and understanding among the participants. A brief history of account planning should be discussed. This history should include the techniques that will be used, results of previous successful sessions, and how account planning has positively impacted customers.

During the session, you should define the customer's business environment and your business environment within the customer organization. Develop appropriate action plans to allow you to help your customer meet their business objectives. The result may be resource commitments and secondary planning requirements.

There should be no reason for participants to take notes, since all presenters will distribute copies of their materials and all additional notes will be taken on flip charts and distributed within three working days of the session.

The "equal participation" ground rule is a must to foster creativity. No one will be allowed to shoot down another person's idea. Everyone is free to contribute any and all ideas, because from one of these will come a breakthrough. There will be no time limits on discussions.

Everyone should assume a management perspective. You are allocating valuable resources toward solving a customer's problems, which should result in significant revenue streams for your company.

Participants should understand that this session is not an event; rather, it is part of a process that is designed to foster the relationship between your company and your customer. Participants will plan specific actions for the next six months and will update these activities every 90 days.

A discussion of the ground rules is important. All participants must understand what is expected of them and how
they should interact with each other. After the ground rules
have been explained, the facilitator should ask everyone to
agree to operate within the ground rules; the facilitator
should proceed only after receiving that agreement from
everyone.

THE IMPLEMENTATION

The account planning process takes teamwork and everyone on the team must contribute. Most inexperienced account planners will allow an account planning session to
deteriorate rapidly into a battle over who has the best
presentation and who should get the credit for the success
of the account. Here is a checklist for building an account
plan that will allow everyone to be successful:

- Diagram the account's organization by business
  unit, division, manufacturing facility, sales office,
  and the like.
- Discuss the financial condition of the customer,
  using graphics where possible.
- Describe the business strategy for each of the
  business units.
- Determine how your company can help your
  customer achieve their strategic goals.
- Describe any installed base or current base of
  business with the account.
- Develop the customer's organization charts. Use
  codes to show who you know and your relationship
  with each person.

- Profile each key contact and identify those people you need to cultivate a relationship with.
- Define the members of your account team.
- Describe the customer's business conditions, industry trends and their competition, key customers, business constraints, and so on.
- List all areas of opportunity that you know of, by business unit.
- List all ongoing projects, by business unit.
- Identify the business units in which you dominate the market. Identify those in which competitors dominate and who those competitors are.
- Develop a strategy (by customer business unit) for protecting your base business, growing the base business, and finding new business for each of your major product lines.
- Develop a competitive strategy for each of your customer's business units.
- Define specific sales action items that will drive identified new business opportunities. Along with the action items, specify the date the action is required, who is responsible, the resources required, and the issues to be overcome, as well as the results. The results will determine our effectiveness.

Use the strategic account management model shown in figure 12–1 to guide the account team through the functional areas of the overall account plan. Once that is accomplished, document the specific account activities on an Account Activity planning form (figure 12–2) as individual activities are completed, and compile the result. Prior to the next planning session, copies of the completed form

FIGURE 12–1
Strategic Account Management Model

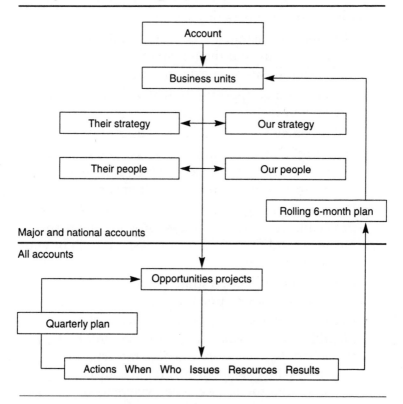

should be distributed to all participants, with all of the results logged. This document provides the basis for the next quarterly account planning session. The activities are checked against the results. If the activities were accomplished on time, there is little need for additional discussion. However, if activities were not completed on time, discussion is then warranted. This is "exception management" at its finest. You are focusing only on the things that make a difference and are not bogged down in bureaucratic reviews.

INVOLVING THE CUSTOMER

The next step is to get internal consensus on the direction you will take and then invite the customer to contribute to your ideas. A great way to do this is to invite the customer to speak to your staff, perhaps at a luncheon, about their current direction and issues. This gives your staff additional information from the customer's perspective.

After the speech, make a short, informal presentation to the customer, using the flip charts you have been working with. Ask for input on how you can optimize the use of your resources. In effect, you are asking the customer, "Is this where we should be spending our time to get the most business from you?"

From this point on, the customer is part of your planning process. Your next step is to become part of his. Having a seat on a customer's planning committee is both an enviable position to be in and a highly accepted one in many industries. It is common practice in the computer industry.

Once customer buy-in is gained, freeze the plan, at least for today. Combine all the information into one package and distribute it to all team members and appropriate executives within your firm. As a courtesy, ask the customer if he wants a copy; the customer will be more open to reciprocate later, when he is asked for a copy of his plan. This builds a solid partnership that can last for years.

Success requires constant follow-up. It can either be formal or informal, but it must be scheduled and completed

FIGURE 12–2
Account Activity Planning Form

Account: **SBU:**

Sales Opportunity	Date	Who	Phone	Resp	$	%	Net	Issues	Resources	Results
		Can Do How To Implement Financial Purchasing								
Plan				Competition					Decision Criteria	
Contingency Plan				Key Relationships					Meets Customer Strategy	

2nd Contingency Plan				Rule Changes					Comments		
Action	Date Req	Resp	Phone	$	%	Net	Issues		Resources		Results

117

on time. As the last action item of the account planning session, set the date and time for the next planning session.

Monthly planning, or minisessions, normally occur every 30–60 days and typically last about two hours. These are designed to monitor progress and to keep abreast of significant changes to the account and to your position.

Update the customer's strategic direction or your supporting strategy as needed. Review your progress and update short-term targeted activities on both the account and specific projects. The last step is to set the date for the next planning session.

STRUCTURED ACCOUNT PLAN PRESENTATION

The structured account plan presentation is broader than the initial presentation given to management to gain approval of this account as a strategic account. This type of presentation is made to show justification for management's continued support. It is normally given at least once each year, using updated information. Here are some suggested topics:

Account background
- Major products and services
- Industry position
- Major divisions and locations
- Organization chart and account team coverage
- Decision processes
- Financial posture

- Description of customer's business
- Major client strategies and your complementary strategies
- Market conditions
- Business constraints

Competitive situation
- Competitor's position, by division
- Major projects you are competing for
- Competitive projects completed
- Current competitive efforts

Account Plan Activities and Events
- Strategic opportunities
- Customer participation in events
- Justification
- Executive marketing objectives

Quota and business volume projections
Plan follow-up
- Quarterly planning session schedule
- Review with client

Resource requirements
- People
- Products
- Services
- Policy
- Marketing programs
- Education
- Budget
- Other

The presentation should be short and to the point. Remember, the managers you are presenting to break their time up into 30-minute blocks. So keep it under 30 minutes; if they ask for more, be prepared to go into detail on anything. If you decide to use an overhead projector, you can use between 10 and 15 slides for a 30-minute presentation. You might use the same basic format that you used in your original presentation and prepare additional support materials as needed. This approach helps you train the audience on what to expect from your presentations and where to look for it. Always leave about 5 to 10 minutes at the end for discussion, and make sure you invite the executives to your next account planning session.

Chapter Thirteen

Planning an Executive Seminar

Many people believe that by getting top executives together in a closed session and presenting them with your point of view, they could get the executives to endorse their viewpoint. That's a fairly straightforward approach, which, by all logic, should work well; that is, if the entire process is thought out properly.

It is this thought process that can be the stumbling block in planning these events. The people in your organization who want the event the most have the least amount of time to become involved and, furthermore, have little or no experience in organizing such events.

The top account executives say, "If I could only get key client executives to believe our story, then they would sell their people on our company and product and our sales efficiency would improve. I think I will host a seminar for a broadbased sell on our products and services." You think the idea is great, and you sell your boss on it, but there is one hitch: He asks you to run the entire program. Now what? You have never done anything like this before. Sure, you have dealt with numerous executives in your career; that in itself is no problem. But what about developing a seminar for executives?

BEGIN AT THE BEGINNING

You now have the charter to organize and present an executive-level seminar. You thought it was a great idea, but now that you have to put the whole thing together, you probably do not know where to start. The first thing you must do is write down a set of concrete goals and objectives. Keep them simple and limit them to only the things that are pertinent. Try to avoid a lot of "motherhood" and "apple pie." For example, one often-stated objective is "Make sure the program is first-class." This goes without saying, or this will be your first and last attempt. More appropriate objectives include: "have 25 executives (at the level of vice-president or higher) from Fortune 500 or equivalent companies in attendance," and "have three major projects secured as a result of the seminar." These objectives are much tougher to achieve than the traditional motherhood-and-apple pie approach.

Here are some typical seminar goals:

- Have 25 executives (at the level of vice president or higher) from Fortune 500 or equivalent companies in attendance.
- Conduct the seminar at a convenient location.
- Select topics that are of major concern to those in attendance.
- Select presenters who are highly skilled, knowledgeable, credible, and effective in their delivery.
- Have attendees leave with something tangible.
- Ensure specific follow-up with each attendee.
- Add three new projects as a result of the program.

You will use these objectives to develop an overall, integrated strategy. During the course of this development, you may also find that you need additional goals to cover what you want to accomplish. It will be interesting to see how many items you add or delete as you go through the process.

THE INVITATION

If you have never produced an executive seminar, I hope your proposed date is at least three months away. If not, you had better reschedule immediately because you will not have time to put a successful program together.

Before the invitation's content is discussed, a color theme should be selected. Notebooks, note paper, and table decorations should all coordinate with the colors of the invitation. Currently, the most popular color combinations are gray paper with gray, maroon, or black ink, or beige paper with brown ink.

The first thought every neophyte has is, "We'll use a wedding invitation format and make this really look important." Think about that for a minute. What is your first response when you receive a wedding invitation? You probably think, "I need to give this to my spouse or secretary so they can buy some kind of gift." Like you, the people you are inviting want things simple and concise; keep it that way.

Try one of the popular color combinations, with several inserts, if appropriate. Also, make it an odd size; anything that is $8^{1}/_{2} \times 11$ inches and white tends to get lost on my desk, and that is typical for most people.

After you have decided on the invitation's color, size, and shape, you are ready for content. If you are careful about the structure and format of your invitation, you may be able to use it for multiple levels of executives as well as for various programs. The areas you should be concerned with are as follows:

The cover. The name of the seminar and an emblem or logo is sufficient; there is no need to put your company name on the cover. That can be placed on the inside. Pictures tend to look unprofessional. Any more than two colors of ink on colored paper tends to look too busy. Embossed or raised lettering will probably triple your production cost, with no real benefit.

Inside Left Cover.   Here you should state the seminar's theme and the questions or topics to be covered. Keep this simple also. Try to use less than one-half the available space, and center the text vertically.

Inside Right Cover.   Here is where the choices begin. If you are including inserts, then you may want to use the inside right cover to discuss other seminars that are available. If no inserts are planned, then this space should be used to state the agenda. When you print the agenda, you may consider printing only the names of the guest speakers. By not printing the names of your internal speakers, you reserve the right to change those speakers until the last day and still maintain your topical content. (You might also consider putting together a list of alternate speakers. A good contingency plan could preserve your credibility.)

Logistics.   Some portion of your invitation must deal with such logistics as time, place, meeting rooms, and transportation.

Seminar content.   Be sure to tell the executive what he can expect to get from the seminar.

Now that you have all of your ideas on paper, do not try to write the final copy unless you are very good at it. Hire someone who does this for a living; you will save money and save face in the long run. When you receive the final brochure from the printer, proofread it again. The first brochure I had responsibility for was proofread by five people before going to the printer, and by five people when it was returned. Even after 10 passes, everyone missed three misspelled words. The printer is not liable for your mistakes; you are!

Now that the invitation is finalized, you realize that there are only six weeks until the seminar. The next section discusses the distribution and delivery of the invitations.

The conversation when you set up the delivery may go something like this:

Receptionist:
Good morning, Acme Corporation.
Sales Rep:
Hello, this is Bob Simpson with XYZ Company, and I need your help. Is Mr. Jim Phillips currently the executive vice-president of manufacturing?
Receptionist:
Yes, he is.
Sales Rep:
Would you please connect me with his office? Oh, by the way, what is his secretary's name?
Receptionist:
I'll connect you with Mary Scott, Mr. Phillips' secretary.
Sales Rep:
Thank you.

Secretary:

Hello, this is Mary Scott.

Sales Rep:

Hello, Mary, this is Bob Simpson with XYZ Company's Computer Systems Group. The reason I am calling is to check and see if Mr. Phillips has May 8 open at this time. We are having an executive seminar on that date in Dallas, Texas. This seminar is limited to executives at the vice-president level and above of the Fortune 500 corporations in America. Would you please check and see if Mr. Phillips has that day open at this time?

Secretary:

The 8th seems to be open, but I will have to check with him to confirm this.

Sales Rep:

Great, would you please pencil in that date for the XYZ Company executive seminar?

Secretary:

OK, but I will have to confirm this and get back to you.

Sales Rep:

Mary, would you also check and see if he has 10 minutes free during the first week of April so my executive vice-president and I may personally drop off the agenda and answer any questions Mr. Phillips might have?

Secretary:

Let's see, how about the 4th at 9:20 AM?

Sales Rep:

Great. I'll call you on the 3rd to confirm. Oh, by the way, Mary, does he prefer to be called Jim or Mr. Phillips?

Secretary:

Jim is fine. I look forward to hearing from you on the 3rd.

Sales Rep:

Thanks again, Mary.

Now, wasn't that easy?

When you arrive for the appointment, it is no different than any other sales call. You must know your product and your customer. Chapter 8, on building relationships, contains 50 questions you are likely to be asked by an executive at this level. You should have an answer for each of them. Chapter 8 also contains 50 questions that you can ask him. Also read his annual report before you go in as well as his latest financial statement. You may also want to give him your annual report as well as recent article reprints about your company published in *Fortune, Forbes, Business Week,* or other business periodicals.

If he elects not to attend your seminar, don't give up. As an executive vice-president, he probably has vice-presidents reporting to him. One of them may be an appropriate attendee. And don't forget, you can still approach the president as well. Of those who commit to attend, approximately 80–90 percent will eventually show up. (This is a good rule of thumb for planning.)

TOPIC SELECTION

Topic selection is one of the most critical issues you will face during your seminar preparation. The theme that you choose should have broad appeal to your audience and should involve current issues. In selecting your topic, begin with your ultimate objective. Just what are you offering each executive? With the average salary of these executives in excess of $150,000 per year, how can you make it worth their time?

People will come if there's a drawing card. Many times the president of your corporation is drawing card enough. In some cases, the presence of a noted authority on the program will suffice. Other times, the topic alone will do the job. Your best bet is to use a combination of these drawing cards whenever possible. If the seminar is for local executives and you do not have access to the president of your corporation, then you should build it around the highest-level executive you have access to.

Building a seminar around a senior marketing executive could be construed as a sales pitch. Executive seminars should be used to impart information and not as a forum for sales. One obvious outgrowth of seminars is attendees' requests to have your staff come in and impart further knowledge at a lower level; this is where the selling begins.

Successful seminar titles include Engineering Productivity Networks, Integrated Information Systems, Personal Workstations in Organizations. Choose your own, but make it appealing.

SPEAKER SELECTION

The tendency in speaker selection is to select the top-ranking people in a specific area. This may be good for your career, but it is not necessarily good for your seminar. Many top-ranking executives are not good speakers. In addition, some senior managers are great speakers but are literally scared to death to do it. Be careful and don't misread them.

The criterion you must use is to select the best speaker, who is not necessarily the highest-ranking individual. A diplomatic approach is to ask the top-ranking individuals to suggest their preferred speakers. If needed, tell these executives that they are more valuable playing one-on-one roles with the attendees than they would be as speakers.

After you develop a list of speaker names, consider holding a competition to see who gets the nod. Use the astronaut approach: Everyone must be trained, but only one can fly the ship at a time. This approach will give you a trained cadre of individuals ready to step on stage at any time.

If at all possible, your speakers should be intimately familiar with the seminar topic. There is a great deal of credibility in answering questions directly. If the speaker can talk about personal experiences, he will be even more warmly received and believed.

If you have a potential candidate who is very knowledgeable but is a poor presenter, and a great presenter who has very little first-hand knowledge of the topic, then use the best speaker available and back him up with the technical prowess of the expert standing in the wings.

Have the speaker go through the presentation several times prior to going on stage. You should be comfortable with his message and delivery style. If you have total responsibility, you should reserve the right to cancel a speaker you are not satisfied with, even at the last minute (hence, the reason for not printing internal speakers' names on the invitation). If you can't get the speakers to practice several times, then at least get them to do a dry run the night before.

The outside industry expert may be even more difficult to find. There are many supposed experts in every field, but remember, you are staking your personal reputation on them and their performance. You might want to look to your customer base for someone who can present a very credible success story; someone who has already accomplished what you are proposing will go a long way in supporting your efforts.

You may also want to consider going to a highly regarded university for an industry expert. If you select an academic, be sure that he or she has been mentioned often in the *Wall Street Journal, Harvard Business Review,* and the like. These individuals' services will cost you $2,500 and up per day, plus expenses. Most of them will talk about what they want to talk about and not necessarily what you want them to talk about.

In any case, the selection process is very time-consuming, so start at least three months prior to the seminar date. Internal speakers should be lined up even before the location is chosen. The external speakers can be selected after the location and dates are chosen but prior to printing the invitations. Good luck!

SELECTING THE LOCATION

The location of your session is also of prime importance. Remember that the executives you are inviting are accustomed to first-class accommodations and service and that their time is extremely valuable.

Choose a first-class location that is convenient (less than a one-hour drive) to the airport. Most executive seminars require that attendees pick up their own tab for travel and lodging, but you will be expected to furnish all meals during the session.

Tour the selected facility completely. Pay close attention to such things as room size, the availability of suites, breakout rooms, and the like. You will probably want to set up the room in a U shape. This is more conducive to interaction, but it typically requires a room that is 50 percent larger than one that is set up classroom style. Go for the additional expense. It will be worth it.

Make sure the facility has an excellent menu. Avoid a buffet-style meal at all costs. Sure it's quicker, but most oí the expected attendees probably hated chow lines in the Army; don't bring back bad memories. Meals delivered individually are much more professional.

When dealing with the facility's catering office, tell them that you want to go first-class all the way. For a group of 35, you can expect to pay about $12 for breakfast, $15 for lunch, and $30 for dinner per person. Of course, this excludes any wine or liquor. Most hotels require that you use their liquor and not bring in your own; in some states it is law. The facility will normally provide a bartender at no additional charge.

You should request that the meals be served at round tables with no more than eight people per table. Plan for a mix of six customers and two people from your company at each table, which ensures that all conversations are covered accurately. So for every three customers in attendance, arrange to have one of your people there also (a 1 : 3 ratio). You may want to increase the ratio to 1 : 2 or 2 : 3, but never allow it to drop below 1 : 3.

Check the meeting-room and the dining-room chairs. It will be a long day, so be sure the chairs are comfortable (with arms, if possible) and that there is plenty of room between them. Do not give the perception that you are crowding people in.

Check the acoustics and determine whether a microphone is necessary. Do you want a podium, a stage, a screen, or projectors? Make certain to determine what type of power is available for demonstrations, equipment, and the like. These details will kill you if you don't pay close attention.

Arrange to have coffee, tea, and soft drinks in the room all day long. Pastry is appropriate in the morning, but nothing is needed in the afternoon. Some type of mints at each place is nice. If you want to be elaborate, you might put a half bottle of wine and a fruit basket in each room when the attendees arrive. Plants are a nice touch and can be rented for the event, perhaps with some help from the facility.

You will need to establish one person in your organization to be the liaison with the facility you use. Make sure the liaison is on travel status; otherwise you will end up doing the grunt work yourself. A title of seminar manager is great for this person, since he is the logistician.

You need to ask the facility to post signs directing your attendees from one room to another. These signs typically take about five weeks to make. One great idea is to attach the arrow on the sign with Velcro so it can be pointed in any direction.

You will need to give the facility the list of people (e.g., guest speakers, the president of your company) whose bills you want direct billed to you.

AMACOM publishes an excellent book for planners: *A Conference and Planners Workshop Planner's Manual*, by Hart and Schleicher. It is available from AMACOM, 135 W. 50 Street, New York, New York 10020.

One week after receiving them from the printer, the invitations should be in the hands of your first-level field managers. Each first-level manager has a filtered target list approved by a second- or third-level manager. It should be the responsibility of the first-level manager to hand-deliver the invitation to the client executive. The sales representative can set up the appointment, but the invitation should be presented by a manager. Whether or not you have met your prospective attendee, this is one tried and true method of getting a commitment.

THE CONFIRMATION

There are several decisions to be made about the confirmation. First, you must decide whether you are going to have the seminar hosted by the president or highest-level executive in your region. If this is your plan, you will want the confirmation letters to come directly from her office, on her personal stationery. If, on the other hand, you have billed the seminar as one that has been put together by local management with special outside speakers, you may want to send the confirmation letters from the local ranking manager.

Included with the confirmation should be the following:

- A map to the location of the seminar.
- A copy of your annual report.
- A copy of your invitation.
- Another copy of the agenda.
- A phone number where the executive may be reached in an emergency.

The initial hand-delivered invitation should serve just that purpose, as an invitation, and the confirmation should only be sent after the attendee has committed his presence. Once the confirmation has been received from the attendee, a list of participants, sorted by company, should be typed, with addresses and phone numbers. You will want to include this in the final notebook that you pass out on the day of the seminar so that the attendees can contact each other after the seminar. From those who have confirmed their attendance, you can expect 80–90 percent to actually attend the seminar.

NOTEBOOKS AND GIVEAWAYS

It is fairly standard that some sort of notebook with data in it goes to the seminar attendees. Here are some suggestions on what to include in a professional package:

- Choose a notebook that matches the overall color scheme that you are using for the seminar. For example, if you use gray paper, then use a maroon notebook; if you use buff or beige paper, then use a tan or brown notebook.

- Some may want to emboss the attendee's name on the cover. That is a good thought, but what if he doesn't show up or someone else comes in his place? You're stuck! A way around this is to leave the cover plain and emboss your company's name in gold on the inside front cover.

- Use a top-quality notebook.

- Have special note paper made. It is not appropriate to allow executives to take notes on hotel stationery.

- Have the notebook tabs printed using the same colors you have chosen as your theme. Do not use clear tabs with paper inserts. They are not appropriate.

- A copy of the agenda should be the first thing the person sees when opening the book. This should be followed by the names of the guest speakers and your company's people in attendance. Next should be a list of the attendees. There should be several sheets of note paper following this. Next, a copy of all slides to be used should go in each section of the book. If you can't get a copy of the speakers' slides, then you should put note paper in that section of the notebook. Also, you may wish to include a biographical sketch of each speaker in the appropriate section.

Be sure to get a copy of the speakers' slides about two months prior to the seminar date. Inserting the data into the notebooks is no trivial task. Do not wait until the day before the session to begin; you should begin about two weeks prior.

THE DAY OF THE SEMINAR

You will probably find that the facility was not set up before you went to bed because the room was in use last night. If your seminar begins at 8:00 AM, you should be on site by no later than 6:30 AM to ensure that all preparations meet your expectations. These are the things to look for:

- Is the room set up as you requested?
- Is all necessary equipment in the room and ready for use?
- Are all supplies in their proper places?
- Are the printed materials there and in their proper places?
- Are the signs in the correct locations?
- Is the heating and cooling system functioning properly?

- Are ashtrays, glasses, and water available in the room?
- Are your speakers awake and getting ready?
- Are name tags and place cards in place?
- Check the weather report for possible impact on arrivals.
- Leave a copy of the program at the front desk and with facility's liaison.

Once you have checked these things, get ready to greet the attendees. You will want to ensure that each attendee feels comfortable. You may even want to subtly assign one of your people to every three attendees to ensure that all of their needs are met. As you move from one location to another, ensure that all find their way and none are left behind. You may want to station one of your people near the restrooms to direct those who have taken a break to the next session.

Stay in touch with the facility personnel to ensure that all the comfort needs of your attendees are met. Give the attendees the name of the facility liaison who can help them with travel arrangements, sending or taking messages, and the like. Introduce them to the liaison.

As the day winds down, your attendees will be concerned about how to get to the airport or other transportation. You should make arrangements for your company's people to escort them to their transportation. Do not allow them to take a taxi.

Another key point is to ensure that each attendee fills out an evaluation sheet. These should be collected by an appointed person and tabulated. It is only through these critiques that you can improve your seminars overall.

FOLLOWING THE EVENT

There are a few logistical things that you need to do following the event. They are as follows:

1. Write a letter of appreciation to each committee member.
2. Write a letter of appreciation to each speaker.
3. Review all bills for accuracy.
4. Collect signs, supplies, and equipment.
5. Arrange for the return of supplies and equipment.
6. Check that all equipment and supplies arrive in appropriate places.
7. Provide feedback to the facility liaison on efficiency of services, and so on.
8. Critique all policies and procedures of the arrangements committee and write a report.
9. Submit the final report.
10. Submit all critique forms to a central corporate location.

By the time you have completed all of this, you will probably have learned one of two things. Either the seminar was so successful in terms of increased sales that another one is already in the works, or you haven't figured out that once you start a program of this type, it is a never-ending cycle, so you had better become very good at it very fast.

ATTENDEE FOLLOW-UP

Now that you have all of these attendees excited about your capabilities, what are you going to do about it? What is your follow-up plan? Most companies get to this point with flying colors, but the follow-up plan is not formal enough to judge the benefits in terms of sales dollars. Here are some suggestions regarding follow-up procedures:

- Pass on the critique form filled out by each attendee to the appropriate district manager. Require that the district manager or area manager do a follow-up visit with each attendee and discuss openly what the next logical step is in the relationship.

- You will find that if you were properly successful in your seminar, the client executive can direct you in more ways than you possibly have resources to handle. That is why it is essential for the management team to do the initial follow-up. This should be the same team that made the original face-to-face contact with the customer. Prior to going in and meeting with the executive, the management team should consult with the managers who were assigned to the customers at the seminar to get an update on the customer's "hot buttons." Management involvement during this process ensures that the sales rep will have the resources he needs to get the job done properly. It also shows the customer that you have an ongoing interest in their success.

- The follow-up meeting should occur within two weeks of the seminar and a written three-month account plan should result. Use the follow-up session with the client executive to show them that you want to have continued periodic sessions with them to review your mutual progress. At this time, also inform them of your additional seminar

opportunities and get commitments on which
additional executives would like to attend.

- Use basic account management skills from here on.

I can't emphasize enough the importance of the follow-up. If you do not do it well, especially with this level of executive, then your credibility is shot and your position is unrecoverable.

Chapter Fourteen

How to Profit from Automating Account Management

With computer prices tumbling, the idea of putting a laptop on every account executive's desk seems like a great idea. Every company is trying to increase the efficiency of every AE, which in turn reduces the cost of sales. The sales vice-president dreams of increasing the productivity and quota of every rep by 30 percent. In some industries this may still be possible, but very few still allow that level of growth. So what is a realistic percentage to expect for productivity improvement with automation, and is it feasible?

The feasibility of automating a sales organization has many aspects, and we will attempt to guide you through the decision-making maze so you can make an educated decision. There are some assumptions we must make, and these will be noted during the process.

ASSUMPTIONS

According to Rowland T. Moriarty and Ursula Moran in "Managing Hybrid Marketing Systems" (November/December 1990, *Harvard Business Review*), "The need to contain costs is another powerful force behind the spread of hybrid systems, as companies look for ways to reach customers that are more efficient than direct selling. In 1990, the loaded cost of face-to-face selling time for national account managers can reach $500 per hour; for direct sales representatives, the average is about $300 per hour. Selling and administrative costs often represent 20% to 40% of a company's cost structure, and thus have a direct effect on competitive advantage and profitability. Digital Equipment's selling and administrative costs in 1989 were 30% of revenues; for Sun Microsystems, the figure was only about 24 percent."

This translates to the average loaded cost of a national account manager being about $200,000 per year and about $120,000 for a direct sales rep, in 1990 dollars.

An average national account manager is responsible for about $6 million in revenue and the average direct sales rep is responsible for about $1.5 million. This amounts to a direct cost of sales of 11.3 cents for four sales reps and one national account manager. Marketing, technical support, and administrative costs are additional.

It normally takes three to five years for a national account manager to build an effective strategic relationship with a customer. The information gathered during this time is priceless and in many cases it goes unprotected. It often walks out of your company in the heads of the people who go to work for your competitors. The time it will take to recreate the relationship is at least one year, under the best of circumstances. If there was a genuine personal relationship between the former account executive and the customer and the account information is sparse, you might just as well start over and expect your investment to be in the millions.

REVENUE-FOCUSED COMPUTER APPLICATIONS

In 1992, Steve P. Hindman, president of Decision Guide Corporation, and Professor John J. Sviokla prepared a paper for Harvard Business School entitled *Managing Top-Line Computer Applications*. Hindman and Sviokla made a number of key points in determining which computer applications to adopt.

A *top-line application* is one that affects the top (first) line of a profit and loss statement; that is, sales. Companies raise sales volume and/or increase prices to the extent that they have exceptional strategic and profit impact.

The impact of revenue-focused computer applications should be quantifiable so that everyone involved understands their worth. Measurements (typically changes in sales, share, and average price) are then translated to (presumably positive) profit impact.

Applications that drive revenue are selected and managed differently than traditional computer applications. The focus is on higher sales volume and prices, not on reducing costs. Applications that ultimately help customers achieve their business strategies are the most effective in producing revenue and price gains. This approach is new to most people and requires new and different thinking on the part of management.

Cost reduction is the traditional evaluation process for computer applications. These applications focus on either direct expense or people reduction and rarely look at the financial benefits of increased revenue.

When a company decides to automate its sales force, a typical analytical approach would be to:

1. Identify all activities that a sales rep performs (e.g., lead generation, territory management, presentations, forecasting, closing sales).
2. Analyze how much time each activity requires.
3. Derive an estimate of the amount of time saved if each activity were automated.
4. Determine costs and project savings.
5. Compute return on investment.

This approach focuses on reducing costs. The greater the cost reduction, the more likely the application will be approved. Projects with little or no cost reduction will not even pass the initial screening under this traditional evaluation approach.

Maximizing profits do not necessarily mean minimizing costs. Increasing revenue is not a subtle difference; it is a different frame of reference entirely. Managers who seek sales increases or price improvements create fundamentally different applications than those who desire cost reductions.

The efforts of a majority of people in an organization are measured by cost control and normally those of only the sales and marketing organizations are measured on revenue increases. Cost-conscious managers do not always understand the financial differences. Revenue or price increases have a tremendous impact on profit compared to cost reductions. Figure 14–1, derived from the work of Hindman and Sviokla, dramatically shows the impact of increasing revenue vs reducing costs of sales. Take a company whose profit and loss statement is shown in figure 14–1. A 5 percent reduction in sales expenses produces a 3 percent increase in pretax profit. A 5 percent increase in

FIGURE 14-1
Example Profit and Loss Statement

		I*	II†	III‡
Sales	1,000.0	1,000.0	1,050.0	1,050.0
Cost of goods sold	600.0	600.0	630.0	600.0
Gross profit	400.0	400.0	420.0	400.0
Manufacturing fixed	130.0	130.0	130.0	130.0
General and administration	110.0	110.0	110.0	110.0
Sales expenses	60.0	57.0	60.0	60.0
Pretax profit	100.0	103.0	120.0	150.0
Profit increase		3.0%	20.0%	50.0%

* I = 5% reduced sales expenses
† II = 5% sales increases
‡ III = 5% price increases

sales volume and price produces a 20 percent and 50 percent increases in profits, respectively. There is much more leverage from sales and price improvements, if one can create them.

PRIORITIZING REVENUE-FOCUSED APPLICATIONS

The most logical approach to pursuing revenue-focused applications is to focus on those with both a high profit margin and a low difficulty of implementation.

Most companies evaluate software projects solely on standard financial analyses such as net present value or return on investment. They rarely factor in difficulty of implementation. It is important to consider difficulty of implementation when evaluating the order of the projects to be implemented. Usually one, two, or three applications will be clear winners in the priority analysis and will be the charter applications for a company. All will have enormous profit potential and will be relatively easy to develop and maintain. In chapter 15, we will take a look at a set of commonly targeted applications for a sales organization and categorize them. We will use a model that looks into your customer's business environment demands.

Chapter Fifteen

Automating the Account Management Process

This chapter will examine the overall environments of an account executive (AE) and the customer and how these overall needs are typically prioritized versus how they *should* be prioritized. The model will begin focusing on the customer environment and evolving toward what the AE needs to be successful. In each case, an application will be categorized by productivity improvement and whether it is management centered or customer centered.

In the first phase (see figure 15–1), the customer and the factors impacting its market are examined. A typical strategic account is operating in a global business environment; their stockholders are constantly stressing improved earnings per share, while their customers are insisting on improved quality and faster delivery. The company's executives are insisting on improved margins and improvement in the strategic relationships with its best customers. It is the responsibility of the AE not only to understand these factors and to communicate them internally but, more importantly, to internalize the information and to set in motion a solid account plan to help their customer successfully deal with the factors impacting their business.

FIGURE 15–1
Customer Market Dynamics and Demands

The second phase of the model (see figure 15–2) is to develop the critical interactions between your customer and the AE. The most obvious area is that of communications (written, verbal, and electronic). In any case, customer communications must be timely and professional. Another form of customer communications is presentations. These must be professional, preferably in color, and easily duplicated across multiple accounts or multiple SBUs within the same account. A solid graphics presentation package must be used in conjunction with such multimedia

FIGURE 15–2
Critical Interactions

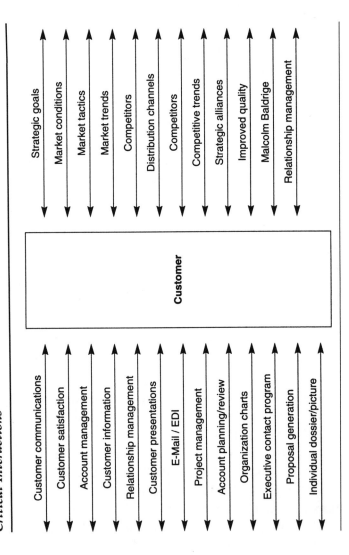

devices as compact disks with audio, and full-motion projection video, or an LCD panel on an overhead projector. Once the presentation is made, the next step is to propose a solution and deliver the proposal to your customer.

Effective proposal generation is typically very time consuming. The more complex the sale the more time it takes to generate the proposal. The more time spent generating a proposal, the less time spent selling. Therefore, an easy-to-use proposal-generation application is mandatory.

The best proposals are the ones that are best remembered. A recent study done by Shannon Blackstone revealed that information printed in Helvetica type font provides a 20 percent improved level of comprehension over any other font. This initial study was further confirmed by Rod Bush, former vice-president of sales for Linotype. Therefore, every proposal generated should be in Helvetica font if possible. With the price–performance improvement of color printing devices, full-color proposals are becoming the norm and not the exception.

The issues mentioned in this section so far deal only with productivity improvements of the AE, which is how most automation systems are justified. While the applications described above may free up an AE's time, thereby improving her productivity, the impact on the bottom line is limited.

The applications that drive the top (sales) line are far more critical than productivity-improvement applications when a company is attempting to justify a large sales-force automation project. Application areas that begin to impact the top line are account management and planning, customer satisfaction monitoring, current customer information, relationship management, dossier, executive contact program, project management, and electronic data inter-

FIGURE 15–3
Applications for an Account Executive

> *Account Executive*
>
> Group calendaring
> Personal info manager
> Voice/E-mail
> Remote access to database
> Word processing
> Graphics
> Spreadsheet
> Forecasting tools
> Funnel management
> Automated approval process
> Compensation
> Forms management
> Sales tracking

Local Processor

---

change (EDI). The question becomes how to equip the AE to accomplish the revenue-generating tasks and make better decisions while improving the AE's productivity. There is a set of tools that should allow an AE to meet the interactive demands of the customer. Figure 15–3 shows a general set of capabilities for the account executive.

These appear to make up a very robust set of tools for an AE. Group calendaring will certainly be helpful in scheduling meetings among several people. A personal information manager will allow the AE to keep track of key people in an account. Voice mail and E-mail will ensure timely responses to customer problems. Remote access to local database information will allow the AE to perform on the road. Word processing, graphics, and spreadsheets will allow higher-quality proposals and presentations. Forecasting and funnel management are very much part of a sales rep's job, and management must know what is going on. Automating the approval process will certainly speed things up. Compensation and sales tracking are the lifeblood of the AE, and forms management will help him keep on top of the mountain of corporate forms that must be completed.

But how do these tools increase revenue? When the president asks, "How much additional revenue and earnings per share am I going to get for this investment?" you may find yourself in serious trouble. The set of tools described for the AE will certainly make her more productive in those areas, but will this productivity lead to additional revenue?

The reason that projects of this nature are justified by productivity improvements is that MIS projects are evaluated in this manner. It is rare that an MIS project is approved because of additional revenue generated. As we learned in the previous chapter, Hindman and Sviokla determined that cost reductions have minimal impact on the bottom line when compared to revenue increases.

Another very important thing to note is that the applications discussed here are designed primarily for individual use and control. But what happens when the individual AE leaves the company or is terminated and decides to erase all the information collected over the past several years? It will cost you a lot of time and money to rebuild the information. Until you have a central repository for the information, you will continue the cycle of rebuilding account information.

In reality, there will be a number of people working on the same account; they must have access to common information and they must all be able to work with the same information. So if our objective is to increase revenue as well as to control expenses, the tools we provide to the AE take on a different complexion.

As you can see in figure 15–4, there is a vast difference in the kinds of tools needed to automate an individual AE and those needed to automate one who must interact with several geographically dispersed team members or managers. It is a cakewalk to provide a set of productivity tools to one individual, but automating the global interaction of an account team and the customer takes a bit more thought due to the complexity of the problem. Let's analyze the tools needed for an account team to operate in a global environment.

Account profiling is the first order of the day. This requires the gathering and tracking of a tremendous amount of account-specific information, such as SBU locations, the strategic direction of each SBU, financials, business graphics, buying patterns, tracking your strategy for each of your customer's SBUs, communicating the account mission, and tracking all team members.

Tracking key contacts in the organization is critical as well. In addition to managing contact information and writing standard letters, you will be calling on these individuals for quite some time, so you will need to build personal information on each key individual (this was discussed in chapter 3).

Market profiles should give you an idea of your customer's market and how it is impacting them as well as how

FIGURE 15–4
Applications for an Account Team

Account Team

Account profiling
Customer organization/dossier
Market profile
Installed base
Strategic account planning
Joint tactical account planning
Proposal/presentation preparation
Sales/project planning
Forecast/funnel management/compensation
Won/lost business
Time accounting
Call reporting
Expense/personal vehicle report
Automated approval process
Business graphics
Word processing/spreadsheet
Remote access to database
Group calendaring
Voice/E-mail

---

your customer fits into your profile of their market. For example, if your customer manufactures and sells tennis rackets, you should examine the tennis-racket market to understand which factors are impacting your customer. You should also examine other manufacturers of tennis rackets to see how they are doing, comparatively speaking. This will put you in a much better position to discuss your customer's real problems—the manufacture and sale of tennis rackets—not what widget you are going to sell them next.

Strategic account planning will give you an edge on your competition because you have taken the time to understand each one of your customer's business units and to think about how you will help them achieve their goals. If done properly, you will have set a specific strategy for each of your business or product groups and mapped them against each of your customer's SBUs.

Joint tactical planning can be implemented with the customer after a solid strategic account plan is agreed to. This approach puts you at the same table with your customer, planning which projects you will invest your resources in to help your customer meet their objectives and achieve their strategies. Achieving this level of cooperation is the ultimate goal, because a customer will normally enter into joint planning with only one vendor in a particular market segment. They do not have the time to do more than one, so if you are the first, it is extremely difficult for competitors to unseat you. IBM has historically been best at achieving this position of working together with the customer to plan their joint future.

Proposals and presentations are critical in any sales situation and should be of the highest quality possible. With the cost of color desktop printing dropping rapidly, color proposals are now the norm and not the exception. This simple expectation implies the need for additional hardware and software to process color.

Sales and project planning follow the proposal or the joint planning session. At this point you have the order and you must deliver it ahead of schedule and under budget. A solid planning system will ensure that you will succeed in this case and will be in line for additional orders.

Forecasting, funnel management, and compensation are the lifeblood of an AE and are management requirements in all cases. These tools will allow management to better balance and utilize their resources.

Won/lost reports are the last thing on an AE's mind when they are trying to close another sale, but to the marketing department this information is absolutely critical to strategic direction and new product development. The best tool would allow marketing to access the AE's information on each sale and analyze won/lost information without the AE's intervention. This again is management-focused information, which will allow better decisions to be made.

Time accounting is required in many industries. This is very much akin to call reporting, both of which give management the information necessary to make more informed decisions. Expense and personal-vehicle reporting are necessary evils required by the IRS. These requirements will not go away in the foreseeable future. Once reports are submitted for approval, an automated approval process will significantly reduce the amount of time required to turn around an AE's expenses and special customer quotations.

An AE will be continually producing executive briefings on companies and key contacts, both internal and external; for these, the capability of embedding graphics will provide a much more professional image in the customer's mind. If expense is not an overriding issue, then the overall account team should have color capability.

Word processing and spreadsheet applications have traditionally accounted for over 50 percent of a personal computer's usage, and this will no doubt continue. Solid word processing and spreadsheet programs should be included among the tools deployed to the AE. As "groupware" becomes a more integral part of the work environment, group calendaring becomes a natural application that would significantly benefit the AE.

An AE should be in front of the customer as much as possible, and that means being on the road and having to communicate remotely by both voice and data. If you are considering remote computing, consider employing a professional in the area. LAN providers such as Microsoft and Novell can put you in touch with appropriate people who are certified in network design and can work with you to provide the best solution.

If your company is like most, you have a lot of PCs and Macintoshes scattered everywhere, and your job is to find or develop one set of tools that will run on both types of machines, with a common database. This is not a simple task, but there is a solution to the problem. Blyth Software in Redwood City, California, has developed the technology that operates on both a Macintosh or PC with a common user interface and common back-end database. Without getting too technical, this is the only technology we have found, as of the writing of this book, that allows a common solution for both PC/Windows and Macintosh environments. You simply take a disk with either the application or the database from one machine and insert it in the other and it runs, with no changes.

With this new tool set, we are now able to accomplish the things that are necessary to significantly increase revenue and to do so in a more cost-effective environment. We are focusing on the things that have the greatest impact on the bottom line.

Now that we have defined the new set of AE tools that will have the greatest positive impact to your business, you obviously will want to see the payoff as soon as possible. So an implementation plan should be set up that will balance a phased learning of new computer technology with the tools required to do the job.

Since word processing, spreadsheet, and graphics applications will represent over 50 percent of the use of the PC or Mac, this is the logical starting point. There are standard education programs already in place from many training companies on specific software packages. You should make arrangements for your staff to be trained formally and not just turned loose with a new "toy." Beginning with the word processing, spreadsheet, and graphics applications will give your staff the confidence they need in the basics of computer use. This will allow them to use the power of a full-blown strategic account management system. They will be able to use what they have learned in this original training in completing the information and graphics components in a solid strategic account management system.

This phase should take no longer than one month, and then you should focus on an area in which management can see immediate payback. Begin with account profiling and customer organization information. You can immediately generate reports that management can see will benefit your people in understanding their accounts. Profiles can be generated for executive visits and lay the groundwork for a comprehensive account plan.

Next, develop a market profile of your customer's environment as well as your market. Next, lay out an installed base for each of your customer's locations. From this information, generate a strategic account plan that involves looking at each of your customer's SBUs, their individual goals and objectives, and how you intend to help the SBUs achieve them. You can do this for each of your own business units or product groups as well.

The sales/project plan is generated after a solid strategic account plan is agreed upon by both your company and your customer. Once this is in place, individual activities must be laid out to move the project or opportunity to completion.

At this point, your AEs will have a good idea of what is required to manage the information they will need to manage their account. The next step is to get them comfortable with sharing information across the network with other team members. This will come initially in the form of the forecast and the funnel management systems. Marketing should be given access to AEs' accounts to review won/lost reports, which should be generated automatically when a sale is closed or lost and should not require any AE intervention. Group calendaring will also get the AE used to networking with peers and management. Call/expense/personal-vehicle reporting can come next. The automated approval process should be an adjunct to this system.

Once the system is loaded and functional, the AE may want to establish her own local database and operate it remotely from a notebook computer. This approach is extremely productive, but it requires significant data reconciliation at the server level when each AE uploads her data.

The final phase is automatic proposal generation. The reason this application is last is that it is very expensive and requires the interface of numerous corporate databases, thereby increasing the complexity and length of the project.

The entire time for an AE to go from ground zero through total implementation and become fully operational should be about six months to one year, depending on their familiarity with automation and the deployment schedule. During this time, a number of significant milestones will show deliverables from the AE to the company that will result in direct revenue increase. It is important to remember that you are not only automating what the AE does, you are changing the way the AE does his job.

Chapter Sixteen

Implementation of the Strategic Account Manager— Automated Edition

The implementation of the strategic account manager (SAM) in an automated environment has been broken down into several logical phases. This chapter outlines the phases and sets expectations of participants. It is assumed that there will be a progressive implementation, initially involving a pilot group of people who will prove the SAM concept. These individuals will normally operate in a stand-alone environment, with the information or account database residing on their local PC or notebook. The next phase is to network 25 to 30 users in both local and remote locations and to have these individuals interact with a central database by uploading, downloading, and reconciling information flows. The third phase is implementation, a general rollout to the entire organization. This will include the integration of information and the interchange with central corporate databases.

PHASE I—TEAM SELECTION

During the initial phase of the project, several team members from both your company and the sales-automation supplier must work closely together to plan the success of the overall project. Team members must be selected from both the sales and marketing side and the technical side. There should be a technical liaison and a sales liaison designated from your organization. Experience shows that the sales liaison will spend his time selling the project internally and coordinating with the technical staff the configuration changes that need to be made to satisfy the business needs of the project.

Many times the total project will not be defined even several months into the project. There are often unresolved issues, such as which type of server platform, notebook, database, network, additional application software, and so on will be used. Change is the norm, not the exception, during this phase and both the sales and technical staffs need to go in with their eyes open to minimize conflict. While many software vendors do not sell "backbone" hardware or software, they are in a position to tell you which have been successful in the past. There may also be a "make vs buy" decision at this point in your company. This is normal and warrants consideration in many cases. One quick way to decide whether to make or buy is to calculate what it costs not to have the solution in place (e.g., $300 per hour times the number of hours you must wait times the number of sales reps in the field). The standard argument is that a system purchased from the outside will not meet all of the needs of the company. No system ever will. But if it solves 80 percent of your problem, you should probably go ahead with the purchased system. Even if you build the system internally, by the time it is deployed, it probably will only solve about 80 percent of the problem anyway.

As the project progresses, a team of users is selected, normally from diverse areas of your organization. This team will configure SAM to meet the needs of your company. It will also serve as the initial alpha test site. These individuals should be leaders in the sales organization and have a great deal of credibility with the rest of the organization. The sales organization should feel that the design of the final system was theirs and not the MIS group's. The likelihood of global buy-in is far greater this way.

Once the user configurations are in place, the alpha software is released to the configuration team. Unexpected problems ("bugs") are noted and fixed during this phase.

It is important that management have input in the final SAM system. A similar approach is followed as in phase I; however, this phase of the project will involve sales management. Management must understand the capabilities they can expect from SAM. During this phase another key piece of the enterprise comes into play. It will be decided which corporate databases will need to share information with SAM. This portion of the project may include a data modeling session with senior MIS people to make certain that the SAM database on the server will properly interact with the corporate databases.

PHASE II—BETA TEST

A diverse group of users from various parts of your organization should be selected to participate in the beta test phase of the project. These people will take the system, as defined and tested by the configuration or alpha group, and move ahead. A training program for both the sales and the technical staffs is delivered. During the beta test phase, someone should serve as the primary support contact for the test group, with SAM personnel serving as second-level support. Second-level support should be available from 8 A.M. to 5 P.M., Monday through Friday, with a response time of two hours.

The server becomes a key part of this phase of the implementation, since users must be trained to upload and download information to keep the SAM databases in sync. The objective of SAM is to build the corporate asset of SQL information in a server database. It is recommended that you select an SQL database that your corporate MIS people are familiar with so they will have access to the database and will be able to accommodate your reporting needs.

Up through and including the beta test phase, the scope of the project will likely change almost daily; this is to be expected when configuring a system to a company's needs. To accommodate this, there will be additional expenses associated with the implementation phase. The number of days should be agreed upon in the beginning; should the number exceed the agreed-upon amount, based on changes in scope, you should expect to be billed on a time-and-materials basis.

During a complex project of this type, you can expect problems to arise. It is especially important, then, that everyone involved is honest and straightforward about any problems and works together to resolve them.

PHASE III—IMPLEMENTATION

A plan must be developed for implementation. A typical implementation plan can accommodate about 120 users per month. This includes equipment delivery, software loading, training, network implementation and testing, and so on. A detailed project plan with resource requirements should be developed for each location and each group of users. A good rule is to plan on one technical person for every 120 users. This person may be called the system administrator and is first-level application support for the SAM system.

As you become more familiar with SAM and how it contributes to your success, you are likely to desire additional capabilities. Make certain that any system you select can be reconfigured without vendor involvement as your business changes. For example, if you change the sales methodology you use, the terms will likely change. Make sure that the software is flexible enough to allow these changes to be made as a data entry and not a rewrite or major modification, which could cost you thousands of dollars. Standard enhancements to the existing application should be included as part of your annual maintenance fee, which normally runs 15–20 percent of list (not discounted) price. A major system upgrade may involve new capabilities and may be priced separately.

Software is generally licensed for use, and ownership is rarely transferred to the end user. In most cases, software source code is escrowed for the protection of the end user. In some cases, source code is sold as part of the deal; In some cases its use is unrestricted, but you should plan to pay for additional users even if you have bought source-code rights. If source code is modified by your company in any way, do not expect the software vendor to maintain the modified code except on a best-effort basis. Even if you buy source-code rights, you may not have the right to resell the code to other groups, even those within your own company. Needless to say, software contracting is a complex issue and best left to those in your organization with proper legal training. When in doubt, seek appropriate advice.

As you evaluate software, there are a number of criteria that may be used. See figure 16–1 for examples of such criteria. As you go down the road to evaluating various types of software for automating the sales organization, you will find a large number of choices and using a weighted average approach like the one shown in figure 16–1 will bring some order to your search.

To figure your data inserted into figure 16–1, use the following steps: Multiply column 2 by column 3 and place total in column 4. Multiply column 2 by column 5 and place total in column 6. Sum columns 3 and 5. The alternative with the largest number is likely the winner. If a "must" category is not achieved by any alternative, that alternative should be immediately discarded. Additional evaluation criteria may be used.

FIGURE 16–1
Software Evaluation Criteria

	Weighted Importance (WI)	Alternative 1	Multiply WI × Alt. 1	Alternative 2	Multiply WI × Alt. 2
Musts					
Runs on both Mac and PC					
Synchronizes with SQL					
Has multilevel security					
Ties Mac and PC to SQL					
Wants					
Management commitment					
Implementable					
ROI <1 year					
Comprehensive enterprise system					
Based on proven account management methodology					

Multiuser shared account information									
Supports complex selling									
View accounts, strategies, key contacts, opportunities, and activities concurrently									
Funnel management with roll up reporting by state/region/product									
Dossier on individuals									
Account planning									
Integrated graphics									
Integrated voice									
Integrated video									
Time/accounting									
Customer correspondence									

	Weighted Importance (WI)	Alternative 1	Multiply WI × Alt. 1	Alternative 2	Multiply WI × Alt. 2
Expense/revenue ratio					
Org chart by sales opportunity					
Multiple associated accounts for each sales opportunity					
Credibility and experience of vendor in account management and computer systems implementation					
Support					
Expertise of supplier in account management					
Multivendor experience of supplier					
Location of supplier					
Training expertise					
Documentation					
Interest in solving business problems vs selling software					

Chapter Seventeen

Summary

I have spent my adult life in high-tech sales. Even the fastest, cheapest, highest-quality, easiest-to-use product will not guarantee success. No individual—not executives, managers, product managers, manufacturing, sales, support, nor administrators—can guarantee success. Success is based on the ability of the entire team to manage the proper relationships. First and foremost is the relationships among team members and a trust that everyone on the team is genuinely interested in the overall success of everyone else.

As a strategic account manager, you must reject the notion of the independent agent. You must demand that everyone on the account team be a team player. You cannot tolerate team members who are focused on short-term business at the expense of the long-term relationship. Account management is like marriage: You have to work at it every day—and even then it won't be perfect.

You must do everything to promote the relationship between your company, your customer, and all the players on both sides, making sure that expectations are properly set, commitments are met, projects are on time and under budget, and sales opportunities are professionally brought to completion. Maximizing your potential as a strategic account manager means tending to many of the details that have been covered in this book. Let's close by summarizing a few:

- Have a good relationship with your team members—including executives.
- Gather meaningful background information on your client account.
- Strive to understand the global business issues your client is facing and how these issues have translated into strategies.
- Build a solid personal relationship with key customer contacts.
- Confirm with the customer that you understand their business strategy and get buy-in on your plan to help.
- Ask the customer to direct you to the projects or sales opportunities that best support their business strategy. Avoid prospecting at low levels.
- Develop specific activities that will carry projects, sales opportunities, and commitments to completion, with accountability for each individual on the account team.
- Move from internal account reviews to account planning sessions involving the customer.
- Verify success points with the customer at least every quarter.
- Continue to teach your team members.
- Continue to learn as much as you can about how to help your customer solve their business problems.
- Manage the process.

Account management is a tough job. There are no guarantees or magic potions, just hard work. The ideas in this book can help you maximize your success and achieve your potential by building on a solid set of processes and best practices.

Account
Planning Forms

Contents

ACCOUNT PROFILE

KEY CONTACT LISTING

FORECASTS

ACTIVITY LOG

ACCOUNT PROFILE
Account Information

CUSTOMER ADDRESS

CITY	STATE/COUNTY	ZIP/POSTAL CODE	PHONE (MAIN)	COUNTRY	SIC	Acct. Code	TOTAL # OF EMPLOYEES

Main Business

_____

Goals & Objectives

_____

Decision Process

_____

Our Critical Success Factors

_____

Comments

_____

ACCOUNT PROFILE
Financials

Sales ($M)	
Gross Profit ($M)	
Net Profit ($M)	
	Sales and Balance Sheet as of
	Assets ($M)
	Long-Term Debt ($M)
	R&D Expense ($M)
	D&B Rating
	Property, Plant, and Equipment ($M)
	% of Sales Spent on Our Goods/Svcs
	Stock as of
	Stkhldrs Equity ($M)
	Market Value ($M)
	Stock Price
	P/E Ratio
	EPS

Availability of Funding

Buying Cycle

Lease vs Buy

Comments

ACCOUNT PROFILE
Account History

Description

_____

Account History

_____

Successful Projects

_____

Unsuccessful Projects

_____

Competitor Relationships

ACCOUNT PROFILE
Market Conditions

Market Conditions

_____

Market Trends

_____

Market Tactics

_____

Key Customers

Distribution Channels

Critical Success Factors

ACCOUNT PROFILE
Market Conditions
Page 3

Competitors

Competitor's Tactics

Competitor's Trends

ACCOUNT PROFILE
Customer's Needs and Requirements

Global Business Issues

_____

Areas of Investment/Growth

_____

Technical Competency

_____

ACCOUNT PROFILE
Customer's Needs and Requirements
Page 2

Channel Coverage

Hot Buttons

Business Constraints

ACCOUNT PROFILE
Strategic Position

Our Product or Business Group _____ Date _____

Base Business Strategy _____

Growth Strategy _____

New Business Strategy _____

Competitive Strategy _____

ACCOUNT PROFILE
Our Sales Strategy

Customer Strategy

How We Plan to Help Them

Top 5 Projects Supporting Customer Strategy

Competitor Activity

Our Business-to-Business Relationship

Personal Relationships

Primary Sales Strategy

Secondary Sales Strategy

KEY CONTACT LISTING
Personal Background Information

Company	Title
	Department
	SSN
	Birthplace
	Birth Date

Bus. Phone Fax E-mail Pager	Home Address

Ht in	Wt lb
Eyes	Hair
Health	
Afflictions	

Company/Location	Position/Responsibility	Employment History From	To	Salary	Reason for Leaving

KEY CONTACT LISTING
Personal Background Information

Responsibilities		Military	
Budget	People	Military Branch	
Revenue	$ Authority	Rank	
		Honors	
Position in Decision Process	Gotchas	Attitude Towards	
		Clearance	

Social Information			
Personality Style	Smokes?	Favorite Dinner Restaurant	
Origin	Offended By	Favorite Lunch Restaurant	
Citizenship	Drinks?	Favorite Food	
Adjectives to Describe	How Much?	Conversational Interests	
	Offended?	Who Buys?	
Cues	Who Advises?		
	Car Type	Golf Score/Hdcp	
Impress Whom?	High Ethics?	Tennis Level	
	Opinionated?		

Education			
Institution	Date Graduated	Degree	Social/Activities

KEY CONTACT LISTING
Family Information

Name	Relationship
	Birthday
Education	Employer
	Honors
Sports/Interests	Considerations

Name	Relationship
	Birthday
Education	Employer
	Honors
Sports/Interests	Considerations

Name	Relationship
	Birthday
Education	Employer
	Honors
Sports/Interests	Considerations

Forecast: From March to May 1994

Summary by Lead Source

Prepared by:

Proposal Date from March to May 1994

No. of Days	Value
<30 Days	50
31–60 Days	0
61–90 Days	0
>90 Days	0

Resp.	Date	Value	%	Description	Product	Lead Source

Forecast: From March to May 1994

Summary by Value Prepared by: ALB

Proposal Date from March to May 1994

No. of Days	Value
<30 Days	50
31–60 Days	0
61–90 Days	0
>90 Days	0

Resp.	Date	Value	%	Description	Product	Source

Forecast: From March to May 1994   **Summary by Responsibility**   **Prepared by:**

Proposal Date from March to May 1994

No. of Days	
<30 Days	50
31–60 Days	0
61–90 Days	0
>90 Days	0

Resp.	Date	Value	%	Description	Product	Source
ALB	MAR 1 94	50	50	TBD	SAM	Mail
			25	Subtotal Net Revenue Forecast		
ALB			25	Total Net Revenue Forecast		

Forecast: From March to May 1994   Summary by Account Prepared by: ALB

Proposal Date from March to May 1994

No. of Days

<30 Days	50
31–60 Days	0
61–90 Days	0
>90 Days	0

Resp.	Date	Value	%	Description	Product	Source
ALB	MAR 1 94	50	50	TBD	SAM	Mail
				TBD		

25 Subtotal Revenue Forecast   Blackstone & Cullen, Inc.

25 Total Revenue Forecast

Forecast: From March to May 1994 Ordered by Proposal Date

Proposal Date from March to May 1994

No. of Days	
<30 Days	50
31–60 Days	0
61–90 Days	0
>90 Days	0

Resp.	Date	Value	%	Description	Product	Source
ALB	MAR 1 94	50	50	TBD	SAM	Mail

25 Total Net Revenue Forecast

Activity Log for:
Daily View for:

Due Date	Activity	Results	Account/Division/Project
MAR 15, 1994 12:00 AM			Planning Forms
Actual Date			

Index

Other books of interest to you from Irwin Professional Publishing . . .

BUSINESS NEGOTIATING BASICS

Peter Economy

This Briefcase Book is an easy-to-understand guide to business negotiating. With seven basic techniques, you are guided step by step through the negotiating process. (175 pages)
ISBN: 1-55623-841-X

THE SALES MANAGER'S GUIDE TO TRAINING AND DEVELOPING YOUR TEAM

National Society of Sales Training Executives

This essential resource includes checklists to assist the reader in managing a staff. It also includes forms for training, planning, and evaluating performance, and gives a listing of additional sources of information for sales managers. (188 pages)
ISBN: 1-55623-652-2